Ancient Egypt

A Captivating Guide to the Age of the Pyramids

(The History and Legacy of the Ancient Egyptian God of the Afterlife)

Maude Garrett

Published By **Ryan Princeton**

Maude Garrett

All Rights Reserved

Ancient Egypt: A Captivating Guide to the Age of the Pyramids (The History and Legacy of the Ancient Egyptian God of the Afterlife)

ISBN 978-1-77485-490-7

No part of this guidebook shall be reproduced in any form without permission in writing from the publisher except in the case of brief quotations embodied in critical articles or reviews.

Legal & Disclaimer

The information contained in this ebook is not designed to replace or take the place of any form of medicine or professional medical advice. The information in this ebook has been provided for educational & entertainment purposes only.

The information contained in this book has been compiled from sources deemed reliable, and it is accurate to the best of the Author's knowledge; however, the Author cannot guarantee its accuracy and validity and cannot be held liable for any errors or omissions. Changes are periodically made to this book. You must consult your doctor or get professional medical advice before using any of the suggested remedies, techniques, or information in this book.

Upon using the information contained in this book, you agree to hold harmless the Author from and against any damages, costs, and expenses, including any legal fees potentially resulting from the application of any of the information provided by this guide. This disclaimer applies to any damages or injury caused by the use and application, whether directly or indirectly, of any advice or information presented, whether for breach of contract, tort, negligence, personal injury, criminal intent, or under any other cause of action.

You agree to accept all risks of using the information presented inside this book. You need to consult a professional medical practitioner in order to ensure you are both able and healthy enough to participate in this program.

TABLE OF CONTENTS

Introduction 1

Chapter 1: Egyptian History - An Overview 4

Chapter 2: Dynastic Era 8

Chapter 3: Myths Of Egypt 24

Chapter 4: The Olympians 33

Chapter 5: Idea Of Pyramids 47

Chapter 6: The Step Pyramid 58

Chapter 7: A Mortuary Temple In The Pyramid 65

Chapter 8: Sun Temples And Pyramid Texts 99

Chapter 9: The Royal Tombs After The Sixth Dynasty 104

Chapter 10: The Unification 124

Chapter 11 Giza: The Great Pyramid Located At Giza 128

Chapter 12: Inventions, Innovations And Technology 133

Chapter 13: Government And Military Power 138

Chapter 14: Mysteries And Secrets Of The Ancients 144

Conclusion 149

Introduction

Egypt has, time and time again, been a mystery to the rest of the world. Ancient Egyptian historical background is among the most intriguing subjects of debate with archaeologists. What is it that makes Ancient Egypt an intriguing area of study?

The numerous pyramids we see in the sandy beaches that make up modern Egypt were built in the time that was Ancient Egypt. In the same way the current Egyptian art, architecture , and literature are believed to originate out of Ancient Egyptian roots.

The present-day Egypt is transformed by various invaders in various points in the past. the rulers of foreign nations have surely made their mark on Egyptian literature and art. But, the literary works and art forms that are a part of those of the Ancient Egyptian period are said to have the taste of the real Egypt.

The Nile valley was settled by one the first human civilizations. This Egyptian civilization was among the most organized and durable throughout the history of mankind. Wouldn't that be enough to give Ancient Egypt an intriguing civilization? There's something else to consider.

The well-known Egyptian mythology developed in these early period. The many myths that developed in that Ancient Egyptian period are still in use today and are an intriguing question to the entire world. These myths form a major element of the myriad theories about the origins of the universe and the end of the universe, and so on.

Are you looking forward to beginning this journey through the story of Ancient Egypt and its numerous myths? The e-book is divided into two sections that deal with the story of Ancient Egypt and the other dealing with Egyptian mythology.

Thank you for buying this book. I hope that it proves to be an enjoyable reading experience that gives you an idea to think about.

Chapter 1: Egyptian History - An Overview

As previously mentioned, Egyptian civilization is one of the oldest civilizations that have existed in the history of human settlements. It is believed to date back to 3100 B.C. The time period of Egypt is divided into various periods in accordance with the Pharaohs who ruled each. The chapter is also divided into various sections, with each chapter focusing on an individual period of the historical background of Egypt.

Pre-dynastic Era

The Egyptian settlement along its banks along the Nile River was possible only due to the irrigation projects and agricultural practices that were introduced in the year the year 6000 B.C. In the early years the Egyptians living in this area of the Nile Valley had also involved in the building of large structures along the banks of the Nile.

The people living in the southwest of Egypt were also making structures at the time, along with the herding of cattle.

The Pre-dynastic Era in Egypt is believed to date back to the time period between 5500 B.C between 3100 and 5500 B.C. The time period was when Egypt was split into two kingdoms: Upper Egypt (Ta Shemau) located in the southern portion of Egypt and Lower Egypt (Ta Mehu) located in north.

In the pre-dynastic period, various cultures were discovered within Egypt. A few of the most notable ones are listed in the following paragraphs:

Tasian culture

* Location: Upper Egypt

* Notable events: The production of blacktop pottery, which is typically an red and brown pottery with black paint on the inside and the top.

* The reason behind this name is that Burials are were discovered within the Der Tasa region located between Asyut and Akhmim.

Badarian culture

* Notable events: The production of improvised versions for blacktopware, use of copper.

* The reason behind why the site is called Badari Site is situated near Der Tasa region.

Amratian culture

* Location: It is located 120km far from Badari site.

* Notable occasions The production of blacktop ware and white cross-line pottery (pottery decorated with white parallel lines that are crossed by a second pair of parallel lines in white) trade with oasis regions Import of obsidian, copper (dragon glass) and gold.

* The reason for the name The name comes from the site of el-Amra.

Gerzean Culture

* Location : Upper Egypt

* Notable occasions: More efficient agriculture that results in a greater supply of food and the construction of homes using the use of mud bricks, using copper for making weapons and tools, and use of silver, gold, lapis and faience to create ornaments.

* The reason to name the site: Location of Gerza.

Dynastic Era

The Dynastic Era witnessed the rule of the Pharaohs. Every period was distinguished according to the rules of the Pharaoh. Information regarding the specific Pharaoh will be revealed in the following chapter.

Chapter 2: Dynastic Era

As promised in the preceding chapter, we'll take a take a look at the reigns and the responsibilities of the various Egyptian Pharaohs in greater detail.

Early Dynastic Period

The Early Dynastic Period marks the reign of the Pharaoh who was the first king of Egypt. In this period that the uniting of Upper Egypt and Lower Egypt into one nation took place. Menes was the king. Menes was the very first Pharaoh of the united Egypt.

It was during his rule that mastaba tombs were built to carry out funeral ceremonies of the dead belonging to the most prestigious families in Egypt.

Old Kingdom

The time period when Egypt was under the rule of the Third Dynasty through the Sixth Dynasty is known in The Old Kingdom. It could be roughly traced back to from 2686 B.C. to 2134 B.C. and 2134 B.C. Pharaoh of this period was Djoser.

In this time the capital in Egypt would be Memphis. One of the most significant events of the time was the building of pyramids that were used to bury the Pharaohs. This is the exact why it is said that the Old Kingdom is often dubbed the "Age of the Pyramids".

The manner in which governance was executed in Egypt was also drastically altered in this time. The autonomous Egyptian states were called "nomes". Each one was run by the name of a Pharaoh. An Pharaoh is more an official in the eyes of the people. He was worshiped as a god and it was believed by the majority of people that Pharaoh was the one responsible for the flood of the Nile and the consequent growth of the agricultural land within the Nile valley.

Sneferu was the first founder of the Fourth Dynasty and propelled the creation of a number of monuments and pyramids across Egypt. It was during this time that the Great Pyramid of Giza was built during this time, under the administration of his son Khufu. In the Fourth Dynasty exhibited highly organized levels of government during the time that Egypt was awash with slaves of a multitude who participated in the building of these pyramids.

The significance in the worship of God of Sun, Ra, increased during the time of the Fifth Dynasty, while the building of pyramids took place in the middle of this period. A greater importance was placed on the building of temples to Ra in the area of Abusir. The decoration of the pyramids was another important aspect during this time. The texts of the pyramids were written inside the pyramids of Pharaohs of the time. The trading of myrrh and frankincense Ebony, copper gold and various other metals that were useful expanded. Pyramids like Sahure confirms the purchase in cedar from the Egyptians.

The Sixth Dynasty saw a decline in the power of the Pharaohs and an increase in the power of nomarchs (governors). Civil wars broke out in this time and a number of minor dynasties emerged which weakened powers of central government. A severe drought was the death knell for the Old Kingdom.

First Intermediate Period

The First Intermediate Period was the 200 years following the end of the Old Kingdom. The rule of Egypt was handed down to a variety of Pharaohs who didn't leave any mark on the landscape of Egyptian time, and the documents speak little about the period.

Pharaohs' rule was from the end in the Sixth Dynasty and the first part of the Eleventh Dynasty. The influence of pharaohs could do not go beyond the boundaries of their nomes in contrast to that of the pharaohs in their time in the Old Kingdom.

A lot of the pyramids and tombs were taken in the early days. This was a time of chaos for Egypt with regard to both climate and society.

The beginning of 2160 B.C. Lower Egypt was consolidated by another set of pharaohs that belonged to the Ninth and Tenth Dynasties. The Eleventh Dynasty based out of Thebes was responsible for the unification of Upper Egypt. The clash with the two monarchies resulted in Theban forces winning the battle and the successful unification of the Two Lands.

Middle Kingdom

The time of Middle Kingdom pertains to the period by the Eleventh through the Thirteenth Dynasty. Mentuhotep II from the Eleventh Dynasty was the Pharaoh who established the era in that of the Middle Kingdom. He was the one responsible in the triumph of Theban forces over the Heracleapolitan Dynasties, and for creating the unity of Egypt. The administration of the civil country was governed by an Vizier.

Mentuhotep III served as the son to Mentuhotep II. He was famous for his visit to Punt that took place during his rule. Fine carvings were a hallmark in Middle

Kingdom art during the reign of Mentuhotep III.

The son of his father succeeded him. Mentuhotep IV. Under the reign of Mentuhotep IV, expeditions across the Red Sea Coast was carried out to collect stones for the building for royal memorials. Because Mentuhotep IV was not married his successor was Amenemhet I, his son-in-law. Amenemhet I.

The capital city of the nation was moved to Itjtawy. The majority of the prior civil wars were quelled during his time as well as the influence of nomarchs was greatly diminished. A plan to gain authority over Nubia was launched during his reign.

Amenemhet II was replaced by the son of his Senusret I who continued to retake the throne of Nubia. Senusret I ruled for over 45 years and was the one who brought stability and peace back to Egypt.

Amenehet III was son of Senusret III and is considered to be the most powerful Pharaoh from his time in the Middle

Kingdom. There was a dramatic rise in the production of food during his time. Utilization of Faiyum Oasis and mining activities throughout the Sinai desert were also key aspects of his reign. Many of the Asians who came to Egypt at the time participated in the construction of Egyptian monuments. The Asiatic colonists were mostly migrants of the Levant region who had emigrated from it due to hunger, drought and violence there.

All good things must come to an end. The prosperity of Amenehet III ended by a failure in the flooding of the Nile that led to the Second Intermediate Period during which certain Asiatic settlements attempted to gain the control of Egypt.

Second Intermediate Period

The Second Intermediate Period coincided with the gradual decline of Thirteenth as well as the Fourteenth Dynasties.

The Asiatic settlements who had made their way into Egypt under the leadership of Amenehet III became called the Hyksos in the year 1650 B.C. Their attempts to take the control of Egypt began with the invasion of the city of Avaris. After capturing Avaris the Hyksos extended their power in the direction towards Memphis.

The Hyksos continued to work hard to take over the entire country in Egypt under the direction of Salitis who established the Fifteenth Dynasty. It was the capital city of Egypt during the Fifteenth Dynasty was Memphis and the summer home for Salitis, the Hyksos rulers was located in the city of Avaris.

The Hyksos consolidated their power in the eastern region of Nile Delta and Middle Egypt However, this did not end their attempts to control Egypt throughout its entirety. It was not until the Hyksos continued to make moves to the towards the south in order to take control of Central as well as Upper Egypt. As the Hyksos were determined to gain power and control, they were also focused on their quest for power. Sixteenth Dynasty was established by the rulers of the indigenous Egyptians who were based in Thebes. Similar to the relatively short-lived Abydos Dynasty was established in central Egypt.

1600 B.C. witnessed the decline of the Abydos Dynasty when the Hyksos began to move towards central Egypt. This was also a threat to that of Sixteenth Dynasty. In the end, Thebes was taken under the rule of the Hyksos at around 1580 B.C. However it was the Hyksos were then pushed further to the north and Thebes gained its independence during the time of the Seventeenth Dynasty.

The Seventeenth Dynasty rang the salvation bell for the indigenous Egyptians. The war for liberation that took place in this time period was successful in eliminating the Hyksos nearly entirely from Egypt.

Ahmose I, the founder of the Eighteenth Dynasty, completed the exile from the Hyksos from Egypt and restored Theban control over the entire nation. The period that was Theban rule in the New Kingdom began with his rule.

New Kingdom

During this period attempts to defend Egypt from invasions from abroad increased in importance and to avoid the possibility of repeating the events that occurred with the Hyksos.

As the time approached for the Eighteenth Dynasty, the wealth and power of Egypt increased exponentially. This Eighteenth Dynasty also witnessed the rule of Egypt by the first female Pharaoh, Hatshepsut. She was the primary reason for establishing trade relations with Somalia as well as Northern Mediterranean region.

Another notable pharaoh in the time of this period was Thutmose III who was also known as being known to be the Napoleon of Egypt. Other notable events from the Eighteenth Dynasty were the expansion of the Egyptian Army and the building on the Temple of Karnak and the Luxor temple, and a temple dedicated to Ma'at, the goddess. Ma'at.

The Nineteenth Dynasty was founded by Ramesses I, who ruled Egypt for a brief time before being replaced by Seti I, his son. Seti I, who led the building for the complex of temples in Abydos. The power of Egypt grew tremendously under the leadership by Ramesses II the Great. The stature that was ascribed to Egypt as a country soared to new heights during his time. But his popularity as a leader could not be maintained by his successors and his period that lasted through the Nineteenth Dynasty eventually came to an end.

The Twentieth Dynasty came into existence at the time of the reign of Setnakhte However, the thing that made it succeed was the rule that was ruled by Ramesses III. Egypt was a victim of invasions from both the sea and the land however, they were defeated as the Egyptian army prevailed. The Libyans as an example attempted to invading Egypt twice during the reign of Ramesses III. While the Egyptian forces repelled all invaders, the wars were costly battles. The nation's treasury was slashed significantly and led to the decline of Egyptian power in the region.

Following the death of Ramesses III the throne was passed to the heirs of his. However, they failed to be successful rulers . Egypt suffered massive drought, civil war and corruption. Ramesses XI, who was the final Pharaoh from the Twentieth Dynasty, grew weak in the face of the chaos. The result was high priests from Amun in the Thebes region becoming the official ruling class of Upper Egypt. The responsibility for ruling Lower Egypt was acquired by Smendes who was the one responsible for the creation of the Twenty-First Dynasty at the region of Tanis.

Third Intermediate Period

While high priests from Amun were in charge of Upper Egypt, they still acknowledged Smendes as King. As time went by and the division of Egypt was more apparent. Priests ruled Upper Egypt from Thebes while the Pharaohs controlled Lower Egypt from Tanis.

Unification in Egypt occurred with the establishment of the Twenty-Second Dynasty, with leadership by Libyan Kings. However, it didn't last for long, and the fighting between subversive groups led to the creation of the Twenty-Third Dynasty.

It wasn't till that Twenty-Fifth Dynasty that Egypt experienced gradual change. The construction of more pyramids continued during this time. A number of temples in the Nile Valley were restored to their former splendor. It was the Renaissance phase in Egypt; Egyptian arts, architecture, and religion were successfully restored.

At this point the status of Egypt as a country was significantly diminished. Allies from around the world were being influenced by Assyria in a single step. It was just an issue of time before the war broke out among Egypt as well as Assyria. Egypt has a variety of wins, but eventually

Memphis was taken over and Thebes was captured.

Late Period

Egypt was susceptible to numerous attacks from the Assyrians which led to the expulsion those Nubians to Egypt. It was the Twenty-Sixth Dynasty was eventually established in the year 1860, with Psatmik I being the king of Egypt. The capital city of Egypt was relocated to Sais. Psatmik I's rule brought peace and stability as Greek soldiers helped Egypt in restraining Babylonian invasions.

In reality, Persia grew stronger as the years progressed and peace was not long-lasting. It was under the rule of Psatmik III that the power of Persia was overwhelming: the unlucky Pharaoh was defeated, and brutally killed by Persians.

Persian Rule

After following the Persian invaders, Achaemenid Egypt can be classified broadly into three periods that include the first Persian occupation and independence and finally, the Persian occupation.

The Twenty-Seventh Dynasty was established by the Persian King Cambyses who was Pharaoh. Egypt as well as Phoenicia and Cyprus was the sixth satrapy of Achaemenid Empire.

In the year the time of 404 B.C., during the reign by Darius II, a revolt led by Amyrtaeus led to Egypt returning to its independence. But, the new independence didn't last for long. It was not long before the Nile valley was reclaimed within a short time. It was in the year 332 B.C., the Achaemenid Empire ended as Alexander the Great began his war on the world. The Ptolemies continued to rule Egypt from that point on.

Ptolemaic Dynasty

Alexander The Great of Macedonia defeated Egypt about 332 B.C. without any difficulty, and the Persians handed over the territory without fighting. The

Egyptians loved the arrival of Alexander the Great while the oracles from Amun announced Alexander to be the child of Amun.

Alexander quickly gained more respect from the Egyptians due to the respect he showed towards their culture and religion. In his time, Greeks were appointed to all the top positions. The city was established and was named Alexandria which was later declared to be the capital of Egypt.

Following the untimely demise of Alexander The question of succession was brought up. After much deliberation and conflict the throne in Egypt was passed to Ptolemy who was the first ruler of Egypt under the patronage of Philip III and Alexander IV. After the fall of Alexander's empire Ptolemy continued to rule Egypt on his own. Ptolemy was crowned King of Egypt in the year 305 B.C. It was at this time that he created the Ptolemaic Dynasty, which continued for a long time to govern Egypt for the next 300 years.

The subsequent Ptolemaic rulers were influenced by Egyptian customs and practices. The problem was that Ptolemaic ruling did not endure forever also. Rebellions, civil wars , and foreign conflicts caused the Ptolemaic Dynasty to the brink by moment it was annexed by the Roman Empire.

Chapter 3: Myths of Egypt

Another interesting feature to Ancient Egypt can be found in the myriad of mythologies that surround the area. These myths were an integral element of the religion that was practiced during Ancient Egypt. In addition they were incorporated into the numerous short stories, literary texts ritual texts and funerary texts discovered from Ancient Egypt. This chapter we will take a look at some of most important Egyptian myths.

Creation

There are a variety of myths about the concept of Creation. They differ in the way they are told particularly in relation to the gods that were involved in God's creation. God. Each city and priest believed in their own God and therefore the god who was involved in making the universe was different from city to town when the story was told.

According to these myths about the creation the whole world was created from the sea of chaos that surround it. The creation of the world from the chaos of the water is a signification of the beginning of life and the emergence of Ma'at. There is also a connection to the gods known as Ogdoad which represent the characteristics of the primordial water. Their actions as gods lead to the sun's birth.

The sun's birth is an indicator of light and dryness in the numerous layers of dark water from which the sun's light originates. The idea that the sun arises from the first mound of land that is dry is believed to have been in the wake of seeing the earth mounds which appear as the Nile flood is receding. In the same way, the first ruler was that who founded the Ma'at.

The stories about the process of creation have changed through time. The later versions of mythology portrayed that the process of creation was an intellectual one. The majority of myths about creation were focused on how the universe was created. However, only a few addressed human creation. In one myth, these few myths, god Khnum created human beings out of clay.

The Sun's Reign God

According to mythology surrounding the sun god Ra the whole planet including gods and humans was under the control of Ra. In the culture of Egypt it was regarded as a golden era that was a symbol of peace and stability. Every leader of Egypt was determined to attain the stability and prosperity that prevailed during the time of Ra.

Another myth tells of an armed rebellion of gods against Ra. Ra triumphantly defeats them, with the assistance of other gods such as Horus The Elder as well as Thoth.

As Ra became older as he grew older over time, humans thought to be the ones who conspired against his rule in order to be the ruler of the universe. At first, Ra decided to punish those human beings who were rebelling but later altered his decision and moved into the direction of his journey to his journey through Duat (the area of death) as well as the heavens. The human beings who were rebelling were later attacked by other human beings. This could be the cause of the war and the destructive nature of humans.

Osiris Myth

The myths associated with Osiris are among the most elaborate and detailed ones to be discovered. At the beginning in the legend, Osiris, who is the symbol of fertility and kinship was believed to be broken up as well as scattered throughout

Egypt. Then, he is brought back to life thanks to thanks to the work of his wife and sister, Isis. The method by the way in which Osiris is revived is a reflection of Egyptian practices associated with burial and embalming.

Isis and Osiris are the parents of Horus, the god of Horus who's life is in danger due to Set, Osiris' brother. Isis is determined to shield their son from wrath from Set and is regarded as the mother of all mothers.

When Horus is competing with Set to take the throne, one his eyes gets ripped off. But, it is rehabilitated through the healing power of Thoth. As Horus is the god of the sky One eye symbolizes the sun while the other is the moon. The belief was that one of the reasons the moon was less visible than the sun is because it was the eye that suffered injury during the battle.

When Horus is made the sole ruler, and restores the order of the world, rituals of funerary that he performs grant Osiris new beginning within the Duat. Thus, Osiris is considered the symbol of regeneration in Egyptian mythology. Osiris is only the ruler over the Duat. On the earth, Osiris is believed to be the main reason for an increase in crops throughout the year. In the Duat, Osiris is the main reason for the rebirthing of the sun.

It's the Journey of the Sun

There are many stories that relate to the journey to the Sun god Ra the most popular one is:

As Ra traverses the sky in his quest to reach the Duat He lights the entire world with his dazzling light. The power of his light is at its highest at noon and then it decreases as the day progresses and the light fades away towards the start of sunset. The stars that shine in our night skies are gods who were devoured by Ra at dawn, and then disperse when the sun sets. Since the sun sets to the west there was a belief that the horizontal line in the western sky was the entrance into the Duat. There was also a belief that the goddess of the sky Nut was swallowed by Ra to ease his passage to the Duat.

Another mythological element that has been associated with the tale that is Ra is the story of the meeting between Osiris as well as Ra. When Ra encounters Osiris the two become one entity. The combination is a reflection of the Egyptian concept of repeating patterns of the passage of time as well as Osiris as the stationary entity and Ra being the active one. Osiris's power of regeneration can give Ra enough energy to continue in his quest. It is believed to have been the cause of Ra rising at dawn with renewed energy, thus giving light to the world. At this point, Ra swallows the stars in order to gain more energy to aid him in his journey.

The birth of the Royal Child

Many myths speak of being the son of God that is final successor to the throne. The first stories were told as folktales , instead of being myths. In the very first of the folktales the three kings who were the first in the Fifth Dynasty were the children of

Ra and a woman of human race. The myth has resurfaced into a variety of other stories to portray different kings as the true successors to the throne. The divine birth of a king validates his right to be crowned. It also establishes the foundation to believe that the king or Pharaoh has the status of a representative from God himself.

Another illustration of this myth coming back during the New Kingdom is the depiction in the reliefs to temples that depict Amenhotep III, Hatshepsut and Ramesses II claiming that their father is god Amun and their mother was the queen of the past. These myths were primarily aimed to give a mythological flavor to the coronation ceremony of the monarch.

The most common theme in all of these myths was the power that the Son of God to restore order to the kingdom and guarantee stability.

End of the Universe

The end of the universe was thought to be as a highly unlikely event therefore, very few books provide a detailed explanation that led to the destruction that is the world. Based on one legend, Atum, the oldest god, will disintegrate the universe and then restore it to its original condition it was in prior to it emerged from the waters of chaos. It is only Atum and Osiris will survive this fateful event. The possibility of a new creation is still present because the universe was formed from chaos and then destroyed in the process.

Chapter 4: The Olympians

After the defeat of the Titans and the rise of the Olympians were the dominant force in the entire world. Their time was full of prosperity and it was during this period that humans (who were nothing more than tiny insects to the Titans) began to develop and increasing their importance.

the 15 greatest Olympians

Let's take a look at each of the most important Gods (who are featured in a number of stories) in greater detail as well as the stories that go with them:

Hestia: Hestia is the youngest daughter to Cronus and Rhea Hestia, the first child to be swallowed, and the last to be thrown out. Hestia was the goddess who was the goddess of hearth. The goddess was virgin, and she had made a vow on Zeus his head that she would never be married. Perhaps that's why Zeus bravely shielded her from the many and admirers. She was a generous Goddess who was willing to give up her place in the council of Olympians to Dionysus.

Demeter is the second child of Titans Cronus and Rhea, Demeter was the goddess for fertility, agriculture and fertility. Demeter also had a son called Persephone who was married to Zeus. When Poseidon attempted to lure her, she transformed into a mare to evade his grasp however, Poseidon transformed into a stallion, and he sat on her. She then was blessed with twins after this incident. A girl was named Desponia. the goddess of horses, and Arion the immortal horse. She had her last baby an ordinary man named Iasion. She was the mother of Plutous who is the minor God of agriculture health.

A well-known story that demonstrates the wrath Demeter is the tale of Erisikthon. Erisikthon was an emperor who chose to build a palace out of wood, and the wood was to be removed from the sacred grove of Demeter. Demeter did not take kindly to this, and cursed him with an endless thirst and hunger, so much that, when his funds was exhausted, he ended up devouring his body to satisfy his appetite.

Persephone is the child of Zeus and Demeter Perhaps, she is among the more well-known minor goddesses. She was known as the Goddess of Springtime. According to legend, Hades was in love with her when she was playing in the meadow along with her friends the Oceanids (the children from Oceanus). Hades abducted her and then led her to his underworld to be beaten.

When Demeter discovered this, she became upset and famined the whole world. There was no growth in crops and mortals began to die. To stop this from happening indefinitely, the gods Zeus and Hermes (there are myths about both) came up with a deal in the realm of Demeter as well as Hades. Persephone was to spend three-quarters of the year to Demeter above the ground, and one-third of the time with Hades within his realm of the underground. This tale was used to provide an explanation for the reason why the plants do not grow in winter since that's the time that Persephone is in the presence of Hades as well. Demeter is mourning!

Hera is the younger daughter of Cronus as well as Rhea, Hera was the goddess of marriage mothers, women, and birth. Hera was also Zeus his wife and Queen of Olympus. Hera was married to Zeus and had three children out of the union: Ares the god for war Hebe The Goddess of everlasting youth, and Eileithyia the goddess of childbirth.

Are you tired of being a spectator watching Zeus bear children alongside mortals, nymphs, titans, other gods, and even on his own, Hera decided to have one child on her own. With sheer determination, she carried Hephaestus completely by herself. After a single glance at him and she realized what a huge mistake it was! Hephaestus was horribly deformed and she tossed his body off Olympus. Being a Goddess Motherhood she had to be a villain was she not?

Hades: Hades was the oldest male Olympian in birth, however, he was the tiniest male Olympian because Hades was the last male to be torn up. Hades was the God of the Underworld, God of the dead, and of all the riches beneath the Earth. Although he was among the oldest Gods, Hades was not in his own Olympian council and was rarely seen leaving his realm.

Hades's weapon of The weapon of Hades from the Elder Cyclopes is the "Helm of darkness" that made him invisibile and unleashed the waves of terror out of it. His kingdom was home to five streams: Cocytus (the stream of crying), Phlegethon (the river of fire), Acheron (the river of suffering), Lethe (the river of forgetfulness) and Styx (the river of hatred).

The Underworld included three levels for those who died: Elysium (the heaven of Underworld and it the Island of the Blest for those who had achieved Elysium during three distinct lives) as well as the Fields of

Asphodel (the place for the average person, who weren't good or bad) as well as the fields of Punishment (the hell of the Underworld in which all evil spirits were).

A most well-known and inventive tortures of Hades is in the case of Tantalus who was the Greek King who hosted the Gods to meals and prepared stew of food items of his own children! In punishment, Tantalus sits in the water pool all the way to his waist under a tree that is bearing fruit, and he is unable to take food or drink! What is the punishment for that?

Poseidon the second oldest child of Rhea and Cronus (either the other way - via birth or through barf) He was the god for the ocean, earthquakes, and horses. He was also called"the "Earth-Shaker". Poseidon was engaged to the goddess Amphitrite However, as his twin brother Zeus Poseidon had lots of affairs as well as many children.

With Amphitrite He had three children: Triton and two daughters, Rhodes as well as Benthesicyme. There were two children with their sister Demeter. Poseidon even sought out Medusa (who was transformed into a gorgon after Athena) When Perseus cut her hair off and her two children, Poseidon, Pegasus (the winged horse) and Chrysoar emerged from her neck. He also mingled with mortal women and fathered a few of the heroes of legend - Theseus The Athenian heroes, Ancaeus, a hero who was a part of Jason and Ephemeus and was a significant Agronaut. It is also said that he helped father the majority young Cyclopes.

Poseidon was a shrewd opponent to Athena to become his God of the sea. God for Athens. He created a stunning saltwater spring, and Athena produced an olive tree for the very first time. He lost by a tiny margin.

Zeus: Zeus was the most youthful Olympian born, however, he was considered to be the oldest (he did not get swallowed.) Zeus is Zeus was the Lord of the Sky and God of Kings. Zeus was married to three women. He had his first lady Metis who he ate due to his fear of an omen that stated that his son would be overthrown by his. Another wife of his was Titan Themis who gave his three sets: Horai The seasons, the Horai, as well as the Three Fates. The third and final wife was, as I mentioned previously, was Hera.

Zeus had many children And by lots, we are referring to a LOT. Zeus' gods children along who were with Hera included Ares, Hebe and Eileithyia. He had twins from Titan Leto; Apollo and Artemis He also had Hermes with the Pleiad called Maia along with Persephone along with Demeter. That's not even his divine children. The family included Minos with the mortal queen Europa, Perseus with Danae and Heracles with Alcmene. He even was able to have Athena alone!

As the god of Gods, the King, Zeus was widely feared by mortals and immortals alike. Greeks were devoted to every traveler or beggar, and even every elderly person they encountered due to the fact that Zeus was known for concealing himself and burning anyone who did not like him!

Athena Then, Zeus consumed Metis then Metis created Athena within Zeus. Meti went to sleep however, Athena continued to grow in Zeus his stomach. Zeus was suffering from a horrible headache, and Hephaestus cut his skull open and out came Athena fully armored! Athena had the status of goddesses of craft, war and wisdom. Athena was a goddess of war, beauty and wisdom. and was never married.

The most well-known tale that is related to Athena was about her battle against the weaver Arachne. Arachne was weaver from Lydia with a unique talent. All over the world would visit her home to watch her weave gorgeous tapestries. In her excitement, she declared that she was better at weaving over Athena herself. This was a snub to Athena and she demanded that she participate in an impromptu weaving contest. Arachne fell short and Athena changed the spider to take punishment for being confident. Today they are known as Arachnids.

Aphrodite The Greek goddess was the definition of a Titan who was born at the time that Ouranus part fell into the ocean. She was the goddess of beauty and love. She was wed to Hephaestus. She was known for having numerous affairs and the most famous was her relationship with Ares. She had children: Anteros (Passion), Eros (Love but some tales suggest that Eros was born of Chaos), Deimus (Fear), Phobus (Panic) and Harmonia the spouse to Cadmus of Thebes and Ares.

Even her husband was aware of her affair, and would often created traps to keep her from being caught together with her partners. He once caught them completely naked inside his bedroom and invited Olympians to ridicule the couple.

She had her daughter, Aeneas, with a mortal king called Anchises. Aeneas was able to survive her battle in the Trojan War and went on to establish the foundations of the Roman Empire.

Ares The god of war was the oldest child of Hera and Zeus and was known as the God in charge of War. The ancient Greeks were not awed by Ares in a large way; after all, who would like the war? There was one exception to this, the town of Sparta. The Spartans maintained the statue of Ares tied to their city, so that God would never leave them, and they would have the courage to engage in battles. It's a good thing.

Hephaestus was the child of Hera by himself and was said to be such a sexy that mother was able to throw him out of Mount Olympus; an action which left him crippled. Hephaestus is the God of forging as well as fire and metal work and took revenge against his mom by gifting the goddess with an throne, which was tied to her chair by an emerald fetter. He let her go after Dionysus had him drunk.

He didn't have children together with wife Aphrodite however, he did have twins who were the name of a sea nymph called Kabeiro and was referred to by the name of Kabeiroi. They were very similar to their father, who worked with him with his forges.

Apollo Apollo's birth Apollo (and the twin of Artemis) is an interesting tale. Their mother The Titan Leto was expecting with twins at the time Hera gave a warning to all the earth masses that had roots to Gaia that shouldn't let Leto be born to the twins. Leto searched all over the world to find a place that would allow her birth and all of them refused. Leto eventually went to Delos which is a floating island that gave birth twins.

Apollo is the God of music, youth, archery prophecy and healing. He also overthrew Helios, the Titan Helios and was made Apollo, the God of the Sun. He was also the god of his own Oracle of Delphi. Even though he did not marry but he did have a number of relationships.

Artemis is Apollo's sister Her name was Maiden goddess as well as the Goddess of wild animals as well as child birth. She assumed the Titan Selene's responsibilities and was crowned the Goddess of the Moon. Artemis was a hunter and had a group of her followers, called" the "Hunters of Artemis". They were young girls who were given immortality on conditions that they remain virgin throughout their lives.

Hermes: Hermes was the son of Zeus and Maia and was a Pleiad. Hermes had a God who played many duties. He was the god of thieves and messenger to the gods, god of travel, sports border crossing, and athletes. After his birth, in an underground cave, he robbed one of Apollo's sacred cows. When Apollo discovered that his cows were not there He became extremely angry. To calm Apollo, Hermes invented the lyre and presented him Apollo. Hermes carried his own Caduceus that resembled the staff of a shepherd and was adorned with two snakes on it. Hermes is famous for his signature winged helmet as well as winged shoes. Hermes was never married, but he had numerous mistresses.

Dionysus was the father of Zeus and Semele. The time Hera killed Semele in order to protect Dionysus from his death, Zeus sewed an unborn Dionysus to his thigh and shielded the child. Dionysus means born twice. Dionysus used to be the God of grapes, wine and ecstasy.

Dionysus invented wine along with his nymph friend Silenus. Dionysus had a lot of followers, and his female followers were called Maeneds. It is believed that in order in order to accommodate him in the Olympian council, Hestia gave up her seat, thereby balancing the male god-to-god ratio of the council.

Chapter 5: Idea of Pyramids

The history of the pyramids in particular their design and design, go through the mythological tales of the ancient Egyptians. As a people it is believed that the Egyptians are famous for their love of death, which is why it's strange that these magnificent tombs were influenced by the story of creation, the story of the birth. 4. According to Egyptian mythology, we are told that the universe was created from the depths of an ocean that was infinite and devoid of life and the ancient waters split with the rising of the sun for the first time. The source of this origin was what the Egyptians refer to as the "first event". The turbulent ocean's lifeless waters the entity they referred to as Nu, broke up into a mound that resembled a pyramid. emerged from the sea. The benben shape was the first part of Earth and the first evidence of life rising out of the water. The mythological images of Egypt was in fact a reflection of the actual conditions of their surroundings that was flooded by water rising from the Nile flood the land but then receding to leave fertile soil with muds rich in nutrients, ready to be sown with seeds that provided Egypt with its abundance and vitality. [5]

The design of the pyramid comes from mythology however, the Egyptians had a variety of reasons for making these structures. The pyramids were used for both funerary and religious purposes and also served as strengthening structures of power for Egypt's rulers. However, the building process also performed a useful practical purpose. Egypt required a huge workforce to provide the food required to feed its population because the fertile soils that surround the Nile required to be managed, crop were tended to and harvests harvested. In one season of the year the agricultural belt of Egypt was covered in water due to the Nile overflowed its banks, resulting in the vast majority of the population in Egypt being unemployed during this time. The construction of monuments was a useful way to keep an inactive population, thus making sure that everyone had work throughout the entire year. Farmers from the Old Kingdom period who were inactive and wanted to work during the Nile's time of floods could earn a salary and avoid taxation through pyramid construction projects. Egyptian citizens who had no other activities to fill their time as their farms were submerged, could build eternal monuments to their rulers with the benefit of drinking wine and beer every day in exchange for their work conditions. [6]

Due to the challenging and no doubt fatal nature of the work that was involved, it's been thought that the Egyptians would not have had to resort towards building their pyramids by themselves. The popular images of the present times have depicted false images of Jewish slaves being beat up as they push massive blocks of sandstone on the wooden logs that were trundling along. As was the case with the Ten Commandments(7, 7) as well as the cartoon Prince of Egypt even featured wood-framed scaffolding surrounding the Sphinx. In actuality, wood was a scarce resource in Egypt that was imported from outside and used as a prestigious product. The Sudan supplied ebony, as well as pine and cedar brought from Syria,[9] and huge timbers were brought in from Lebanon to build ships. The deficiency of timber in the dry regions in Egypt caused the fringe theorist Erich von Daniken to conclude that aliens were responsible for the creation of these magnificent structures and has been a source of inspiration in popular culture through TV shows such as Doctor Who [11], as as TV and film series like Stargate. 12 "The blocks of stone used for construction" von Daniken stated, "were transported on rollers. Also, they were wooden rollers! However, the Egyptians could not have cut down and made rollers of the handful of trees, mostly palms that (as currently) were growing in Egypt due to the fact that dates from palms were essential for food , and the fronds and the trunks were the only thing that provided shade to the dry ground. They must be wooden rollers or else there wouldn't even be the most flimsiest scientific explanation for the construction of the pyramids."[13]13

Von Daniken's main argument regarding the accomplishments of the past is that human beings did not have the capability to achieve these feats and therefore were not the primary reason for the great ancient monuments. He suggested a more future where space travellers and possibly native Martians trying to escape the changes in the environment on their home planet, flew and landed on Earth and brought vast amount of information and technologies together. 14 Von Daniken theorized that "a group of Martian giants may have fled to Earth to establish the new homo sapiens through mixing with the semi-intelligent species living on Earth... gigantic beings who came from the stars and could move huge stones and taught men techniques that were not yet discovered on Earth and who eventually passed out."[15]15

But, it is now an occupation to understand the potential of these kinds of construction projects through reconstructive techniques which rely on the established construction conditions and the experiences from the past. The archaeological research revealed that although wood was scarce however, one thing Egypt was able to get plenty of at the period of the Nile flooding was the mud. By using mud bricks in the form of ramps of mud could allow limestone block to be pulled and towed along the slippery surface of wet ramps. The same experiments have been used to calculate the building period of pyramid construction. Although they're not conclusive to prove that the techniques used in earlier times, these experiments definitely provide a glimpse of the methods that Egyptian craftsmen might have employed. A different theory suggests that the building process was divided into two ramps, one of which was the inner. As that outer ramp was eliminated and the inner ramp was made an integral part of the structure. [17]

The history of pyramid construction was one that lasted for a long time in the past of Egypt that lasted for many centuries in which techniques were developed and evolving, but then being forgotten and lost. In the end that, as the generations after created new, large-scale construction projects that transformed the landscape of Egypt and the world, they did it in a variety of ways.

The first royal tombs in Egypt were found in Abydos located in the region called Umm el-Qaab. Cemetery U , which is located in the first area of the Abydos cemetery, which includes graves dating to Naqada I, II and III periods. This is the place where the first Egyptian burial tombs of the royal family were built and were the predecessors of those of the First and Second dynasties.

The most treasured of these earlier tombs was the tomb U-J. It was discovered by Amelineau in the early 1900s, the tomb, as well as the Umm el-Qaab area has more recently been the subject of an German operation under the direction under the direction of Gunter Dreyer. The tomb had various grave goods, such as imported wine jars, ivory tags that contained some of the first evidences for Egyptian writing. However, the design of the tomb was rectangular divided into twelve chambers and constructed of brick. The tomb was probably topped by wooden beams encased in mats and bricks, with a tumulus which is also known as burial mound. The mound could be symbolic of the primordial mound from which life was first conceived in the old Egyptian myths. By making a symbol out of this mound, it could be that the tomb owner was trying to be reborn during the afterlife. [22]

Following the burials in cemetery U and cemetery U, additional royal tombs were constructed at Abydos. The royal cemetery was discovered by Amelineau and later Petrie, who soon realized the significance of these massive tombs. The entire ruling families during the First Dynasty and the last two rulers of the Second Dynasty built their tombs in the region in Umm el-Qaab at Abydos,[24] and each tomb is distinct since the rulers of that period constantly re-inventing their ideas of what a royal tomb ought to appear to be. In this time, rulers also constructed temples or funerary enclosures, close to the city of Abydos located in what is that is now called Abydos's North cemetery. The most well-known of these is the one of the king Khasekhemwy because of it being the only enclosure that has remained as an impressive structure up to the present today.

The remains of the tomb of Khasekhemwy.

The earliest burial grounds at Abydos included pyramids however they were magnificent structures on their own and contained numerous elements that were later incorporated into the complexes of pyramids from those of the Old as well as the Middle Kingdoms. For instance the royal tombs at Abydos was surrounded by rows of subordinate graves that were surrounded by it, just as later tombs around the king's pyramid. In later times the tombs were used reserved for relatives and high officials who desired to be buried next to the king. Their tombs being prepared ahead of time in case they were to die. The predynastic period was when these graves in the secondary burials provide evidence of human sacrifices which were sent by the king to the afterlife. [25]

Funerary enclosures contained components that later would be discovered within pyramids. In particular, in the enclosures were boats that were that were buried in sand. These burials of boats were also found in the tombs of the monumental high officials of the time in Saqqara and were similar to the burials of boats with kings in later times. One of the most famous boat burials was of Khufu which is one of the vessels is on display within its very own museum in Giza. These boats could be used in the first funerary procession, and were burial with the king to commemorate his journey to the afterlife.

The funerary enclosure at Khasekhemwy the mound was located in a similar location as a mound found in the enclosure of the pyramids that was built by the King Djoser located at Saqqara. It is possible that the mounds were used in the same way and may have been part of earlier structures in Abydos. Some have referred to this mound as one that is a "proto-pyramid structure."[27]It is believed that Djoser converted the mastaba burial site into the step pyramid just half century after the enclosure for Khasekhemwy's funerary was constructed.

A mastaba

Chapter 6: The Step Pyramid

The Third Dynasty was possibly founded by King Nebka, however, Netjerikhet, his successor, were likely to be connected to Second Dynasty rulers buried at Abydos. Netjerikhet, however, is more often referred to as King Djoser, well-known because of the Step Pyramid at Saqqara. Saqqara's Step Pyramid was not only the first pyramid found in Egypt It was also the first massive burial chamber made of stone in Egypt. [31]

This structure was originally planned as a mastaba, however the layout of the monument passed through several stages. The designer of the tomb is famous Imhotep who was later worshipped as the god of wisdom in late in the Late Period. The work of Jean-Philippe Lauer's meticulous excavations and research of the ancient pyramid, we have learned that the structure itself was at least four distinct phases that included a mastaba, a greater mastaba and a smaller step pyramid, and then the taller stepped pyramid we see in the present. This pyramid is six-step 60-meter tall structure. The underground rooms of the pyramid have chambers that are decorated with blue faience tiles, which symbolize the cycle of renewal and rebirth, as well as the burial chamber of granite.

The actual structure was one element of a larger complex of pyramids. The design of this new structure the earlier design elements were replicated in stone. [34] In doing so the structures that were usually temporary were made permanent. The large niched wall surrounds a massive rectangular space measuring 277 x 544 metres. The entry point into the compound is located at the southernmost point of the east-facing wall. The courtyard in the southern part was most likely a court for festivals, including the two "turning markers" that was the place the place where the King's "run" took place. [36]It is believed that South from this is south of this was the "South tomb,"" an additional model of burial location for the King (complete with the burial chamber of pink granite) which may have once contained one of the burials of statue of kA. The east of the court for festivals, there is an area with 25-30 chapels dedicated to gods from all over Egypt. The court is probably connected to, or perhaps it is the site of the King's Sed festival. [39]

A photo of temples in the vicinity of the complex

A photograph of a reconstruction of the corridor leading to the entry point of the Step Pyramid. Step Pyramid

The pyramid's north is a temple-like building, possibly an early predecessor to later pyramid temples. The temple has an area for purification, possibly to be used for rituals or simply purifying the priests prior to entry into sacred spaces as well as false doors as well as the cult statue of the King. [41]

After Djoser developed this innovative type of massive burial chamber, the royal tomb soon became a standard type of tomb for kings, at least theoretically. Many of the successors of Djoser's designed massive step pyramids, but none of the kings of the third dynasty was capable to construct one. [42]

Sekhemkhet built his pyramid from southwest of Djoser's. He designed an area that would eventually be similar to the dimensions of the Djoser complex. The two structures are very similar in appearance in several ways. The site may be inspired by the Djoser's Pyramid, however, the structure was near to the royal tombs of earlier times dating back to in the Second Dynasty. The wall that surrounds the enclosure is adorned with a graffito of Imhotep and suggests that the official might have been involved in the development of the complex, as well. The pyramid and its superstructure were abandoned before they were completed, possibly because of the king's brief period of rule. [45]

When he explored the surrounding area of the pyramid by Goneim, he discovered tunnels to the north of the pyramid, which leads underneath and over the pyramid, to the tomb. In the tunnel, he discovered bones of animals sacrificed as well as demotic papyri dating to the Twenty-Sixth Dynasty, as well as an Third Dynasty "treasure trove." There were a variety of stones, twenty-one bracelets, tiny mussel shells and faience corals encased with gold leaf, which made it the most extensive collection of prehistoric Egyptian jewels made from gold. Seal impressions found in underground rooms verify that the structure was constructed to be used by Sekhemkhet. The burial chamber was an unopened, sealed, Egyptian alabaster sarcophagus. [47]

A photo of Sekhemkhet's Pyramid of Sekhemkhet

Zawiyet el-Aryan is a site south of Saqqara located half way across Giza and Abusir and Abusir, which was the site of the planned Third Dynasty pyramid as well. There are two unfinished pyramids in this area, however, the larger unfinished pyramid could have been owned by Khaba, the Third Dynasty king Khaba who was only in power for six and seven months. The attribution is based at least partly, on the discovery of eight vessels made of alabaster in the north of the pyramid, with Khaba's name on the vessels. Based on the limited evidence available, certain Egyptologists have suggested that there are other people as the owners of the pyramids like Neferka or another Third Dynasty king. The design of the pyramid is in between Sekhemkhet located at Saqqara and the Pyramid at Snefru at Meidum and, therefore, whatever who the proprietor is it's likely to be from the Third Dynasty. [50]

New Heights

The first King from the Fourth Dynasty, Snefru, was the first king to construct the first true pyramid. Like many great inventions the new form of architecture wasn't created in a flash. In his quest to construct the ideal tomb for himself, Snefru constructed four pyramids that include one in Meidum and another in Seila and two in Dahshur. Of them three, there is only one that Dahshur's Red Pyramid of Dahshur is the only true pyramid. In addition to enhancing the shape of the pyramid Snefru also altered the elements within the overall design of the surrounding areas of the pyramid and created a brand new kind of complex pyramid.

The pyramid of Meidum

Chapter 7: A mortuary temple in the pyramid

Before we go over each of these four pyramids the general changes to pyramid complexes need to be discussed. Under Snefru the complex of pyramids was reoriented to the east-west direction instead of north-south. In this new direction, the pyramid temple was relocated towards the east side of the pyramid. Previously, previously they were located on the northern face of the pyramid. The temple complex in its entirety was now accessed from the east that connected to a causeway that then was a temple in a valley. The temple was closer to the area of cultivation than the pyramid in the desert. A smaller satellite pyramid was built in the south of the main pyramid, which could be being the successor to the former South Tomb. It is believed that these modifications were influenced by the prominence to the god of sun Ra (hence that the orientation of east and west). It is probable that God Osiris was already playing an important role in the story. [51]

Seila: Seila pyramid is among the least popular of Snefru's monuments. It was not designed to function as a tomb, nor was it ever intended to serve as the final burial site. It's a simple step pyramid that has no chambers in its structure. The only identifier for the structure was the remnants of an offering table, and an stela made of limestone that permitted excavators to recognize the ruin that belonged to Snefru. [52It is believed that Seila is one of seven tiny step pyramids scattered across Egypt. Architecturally, these seven pyramids can all be traced back to the late Third Dynasty to the early Fourth Dynasty (reign of Snefru). There could have been other pyramids constructed, such as one in Benha (ancient Athribis) in the Delta that was evident in the nineteenth century. Theories about the purpose or significance of these pyramids differ widely however there is no consensus on the matter. [54]

It is believed that the Meidum pyramid was originally designed as a seven-step structure, but it was expanded into eight step. At the end of the third stage of construction, an effort was made to change the structure into a real one with smooth sides however, the changes were not stable. The entry point into the pyramid remained in line with the standard north-south approach prevalent in the Third Dynasty, but the entryway was positioned high on an upper part of the superstructure's north side. It was an unusual feature in step pyramids. The mortuary temple in this particular pyramid is also unique. It was the first one to be constructed on the east-facing side of a pyramid. It was found to be almost intact. This is the best preserved temple dating from in the Old Kingdom. It has a square floor design and comprises an entryway and an open courtyard and then the room has two stelae, as well as the offering table. The stelae are not adorned with designs or inscriptions, probably because of a absence of religious reasons. Graffiti found in the temple dates from the earliest times to present day including that of the Eighteenth Dynasty of the New Kingdom. Near the southwest part of the temple was a tiny pyramid, which was the oldest known cult pyramid , and the next-in-line of the South Tomb. Mastabas close to the structure of the pyramid were probably intended to be used by family members of the King. The Meidum Pyramid was destroyed towards the end of New Kingdom, leaving the fragments of the central structure which we have in the present. [57]

One of the two Dahshur pyramids is most likely his most well-known, The Bent Pyramid. Its unique shape was due to the architects recognizing an error in the original plan while creating what was supposed to be the first real pyramid. The initial plan was to build an elongated pyramid that had a 60-degree angle. This angle was changed until it was less than 55 degrees and finally, at 45 degrees. This final adjustment is what creates the pyramid's bent form. It was likely altered to reduce the size and weight of the top and the lower part of the structure, eliminating the danger of damaging any chambers within it. The pyramid is accessed via a northern entrance that is 12 meters above the ground and another entrance in the western part that is 30 meters higher than the ground. The chambers and corridors accessible through these two entrances were joined with a narrow and irregular tunnel cut into the core of the pyramid. The two systems in combination provide the traditional north-south orientation for the substructure, which includes the burial chamber, as well as the new east-west arrangement of the complex. Stadelmann [58] also suggests that this may be the start of the three-chamber section of the substructure, which would be the norm for future pyramids. One of the chambers that is accessible from the west entryway carried an image of Snefru who was identified as the person who constructed the pyramid.

A stela in the chapel of offering near the pyramid also has Snefru's Cartouche, further supporting his ownership of the pyramid. [59]

Images from the Bent Pyramid

As we mentioned before in the previous paragraph, the Bent pyramid was beginning to include the new orientation of east-west for the complex of pyramids. The chapel on the north was built on its north-facing wall. Based on models from later times it could have been tiny brick structure that had an altar. On the east side that was the pyramid, there was an open cult church in which the stela bearing Snefru's name and his titles was discovered. The chapel underwent numerous renovations, and continued to help Snefru's cult throughout his time in the Middle Kingdom. A small cult temple was located on the south side of the principal pyramid, and included an offering area on the east-facing side. A massive limestone wall was erected around all of the complex. The causeway into the valley temple wasn't paved but was laid with limestone blocks and surrounded by small, rounded stones. It is among the earliest known valley temple that has been discovered archaeologically. The temple was constructed of fine white limestone, and was rebuilt during its Middle Kingdom period. The design of the temple has three equal sections with the middle one being an outdoor court. The southern portion has storage rooms and wall scenes of a procession funeral estates that were portrayed as a personification, offering offerings to the King. The north section includes the portico, which is adorned with limestone pillars that are in two rows decorated with pictures of the king's participation in the Sed celebration. Beyond the portico are six niches that each contained the image of the King. The temple was enclosed by a wall of mudbricks, and between the both the wall and temple was the homes of priests belonging to Snefru's funeral cult that lasted until the Middle Kingdom. [61]

The Red Pyramid of Dahshur was Snefru's last pyramid and was the first "true" pyramid found in the ancient Egypt. It was in this particular pyramid that Snefru was believed to be burial site, just four kilometers from the earlier Bent Pyramid. The name of the pyramid comes due to the red limestone at its central area, which is visible due to its white limestone casing that is almost totally gone. The pyramid was constructed at the lowest point of any Egyptian pyramid - possibly to prevent the difficulties that plagued Bent Pyramid. Bent Pyramid. The blocks from Tura limestone was used as the foundation and for the casing. Builders' inscriptions were discovered on the blocks of the casing and in the core providing dates that can aid archaeologists in reconstructing the chronology of the construction of the pyramid. The entry point into the pyramid is situated on one of the walls on its northern side. It is which is twenty-eight meters above the level of the ground. The corridor connects to two antechambers; the second one with an entrance into the burial chamber, which is eight meters higher than the floor. While the antechambers face south-north, the burial room is oriented east-west for first time in an edifice.

Although the pyramid was finished when the king Snefru passed away and had to be buried, other structures within the complex of pyramids did not. A mortuary temple was constructed however only a tiny part of it is left. There was no cult pyramid built and the causeway not completed. There were pathways and supply roads that ran towards Nile Valley. Nile Valley, but these could have been functional because they ran toward the town of the pyramid. [64]

Giza

The layout of Giza

Giza's Great Pyramid Great Pyramid of Giza, also called Giza's Pyramid of Khufu

One of the stones used for casing in Giza's Great Pyramid of Giza

A photograph of a seal of clay discovered in the pyramid, with its name Khufu on it.

Snefru had a son named Khufu and is referred to in the present as Cheops who built Giza's Great Pyramid of Giza. Although we don't have any historical facts from the time of Khufu's rule the massive structure has made him famous both in the past and in the contemporary world. In the tomb, burial was located within the center part of the pyramid not beneath it or at the level of the ground. Valley temples, the pyramid temple, causeway and valley initially had relief decorations celebrating Egyptian values of kingship and commemorating the king's death. These reliefs are lost , a stunning remains of the complex is the huge wooden funerary boat that was buried in a pit located just from the southern part of the pyramid. The boat is now meticulously restored and is now situated at its very own Museum. The pits of boats are a typical element of pyramids, and Khufu's had five of them - the boat just happened to be exceptionally well preserved. The east side from the principal pyramid are three smaller pyramids that were dedicated to the Khufu's Queens. To the east, was found an amazingly intact graveyard products for Queen Hetepheres. mother of King Khufu. The body of the queen was not found however the furniture found is among the most ancient of its kind in existence. The overall size of Khufu's funerary structure could make it one of 7 wonders in the world. It may also have helped later generations in depicting King Khufu's image as one of a brutal and tyrant with a smear of cruelty. [65]

Khufu's son [66 as well as his successor Radjedef and his pyramid was in Abu Rawash and not at Giza the monument will be addressed in the next section. Following Radjedef Khufu's second son, one of his sons took over the throne. Khafre was the king. Khafre built his pyramid after the one of his father, but on the smaller scale, however, on higher ground so that it appeared to be to be the same. Khafre's Pyramid Complex also features the famous Sphinx that is a huge human-headed lion, carved out of the bedrock. In later times the majestic statue was regarded as god and being worshipped by the Eighteenth Dynasty king Thutmose IV blaming his rule on the vision God gave him. [68The area in close proximity to the Sphinx was a structure that was thought as a prelude to The Fifth Dynasty sun temples[69] (discussed below).

It is the Pyramid of Khafre

Menkaure's pyramid in the vicinity was smaller than Khufu or Khafre however, it was constructed with higher-end building materials, which included a huge volume of granite. His structure was near the other two which made it an important third among the Giza pyramids. The new style of smaller pyramids started by Menkaure was to be carried on throughout the remainder of the Old Kingdom. It appears that Menkaure could not complete his complex of pyramids on his own, and was completed by the son of his successor and successor Shepseskaf. Before we get into the details of the tomb of his father, we will begin by looking back at Radjedef.

Pyramid of Menkaure

Radjedef was, as mentioned earlier was Khufu's successor and was likely to be the brother of Khafre. While he was not able to create his own tomb within his father's Great Pyramids of Giza, there was a pyramid that he constructed in Abu Rawash and finished parts of his father's compound in Giza. [71] Despite his brief time in office, Radjedef did have one notable mark on the past as he was the very first King to use the name "Son of Ra" and in reference to the same god in his personal name. The epithet would be a common epithet in the royal title of all Egyptian rulers during to the Roman period. The god Ra was also to become very important in funerary religions as was being observed by the modifications to the pyramids in this period.

The Radjedef pyramid complex wasn't covered in Tura limestone, which is similar to those of the Giza monuments. Instead, it instead covered with granite. The cult complex to the east of the pyramid featured granite columns, and was lined with basalt. It was believed that the pyramid and complex were not completed, however the more recent excavations at the site suggests that it was not. Indeed, recent excavations suggest that Radjedef who was believed to be only reigning for six years, actually ruled for more than twenty years. The complex of cults is unique in its layout from any other Old Kingdom mortuary temple. A smaller pyramid was found in the southwest part of the complex, and was found to hold some funerary objects for queens. While it's not known whether the pyramid was initially intended to be used to be a burial site for queens but it certainly was used as a burial site for a queen. She was probably married to Radjedef and was a daughter of Khufu Based on the materials discovered. There were a number of statues discovered at the site, including the first known royal sphinx, which was a smaller version of Giza's Great Sphinx of Giza.

After the completion of the pyramid built by his father, Shepseskaf oddly chose not to construct a pyramid for himself. Instead, he chose an enormous mastaba in South Saqqara, today known as Mastabat el-Fara'un. The mastaba is located towards the south-west and is built of limestone. The casing was mostly made of white limestone with the bottom stage of pink granite. Certain casing blocks are engraved with the name of prince Khaemwaset from the Nineteenth Dynasty, a son of Ramses II, who claimed to have restored the monument, as well as others. The mortuary shrine probably was constructed a little because it served as an ad-hoc mastaba and still retain certain of the functions that were of the temples within the pyramid complexes. The temple was located north-south and was on the east end of the mosque. The causeway that connected the complex was located at the southeast end of the temple, and then along the south wall and then into the courtyard. This tomb is distinctive not just for its design but also because it is totally isolating. There are no burials nearby of Shepseskaf's family members or high-ranking officials. It's also not clear what motivated him to construct his grave so far from his father's tomb at Giza However, it is possible that this decision could have been motivated by a desire to bind his tomb to the Snefru pyramids in Dahshur that were located just from the new location. Shepseskaf's reign was brief and therefore there may had been plans for an even larger complex, plans that were abandoned after it was the Fourth Dynasty ended. The tomb contained certain features that were later preserved in the future by successors to his. The burial chamber, which had an elongated ceiling made of slabs was to be the foundation for future royal tombs as well as the temple of the statue was the very first with a fake door. [77]

The Fifth Dynasty

After the close of Fourth Dynasty, pyramid complexes were standardized. The pyramids were smaller than those of their predecessors However, the kings also concentrated on other religious elements of the funerary religion including temples, and especially those that were associated with the sun worship. The first King from the Fifth Dynasty was Userkaf. His connections to the previous Dynasty is not clear, but it is fascinating that an ancient Middle Kingdom story describes him as well as the two kings who followed him as brothers who were all being born into the marriage of a priest to sun god Ra. The story is not likely to be accurate however it shows that centuries later, the significance of the worship of Ra in this time was rediscovered. In the next section, we'll examine the different pyramids from the 5th and 6th Dynasties, then two different features of the royal mortuary religion of the time of the sun temples and pyramidal texts.

Userkaf built his complex of pyramids in the northern part of Saqqara near his Step Pyramid. The pyramid complex didn't yet have the arrangement that later complexes feature. The pyramid was probably constructed in horizontal layers like the pyramids built by the later Fifth Dynasty kings. The entry point to the pyramid was on the courtyard's pavement just in front of the north walls of the pyramid. It is not usual that the principal mortuary temple is located situated on the south of the pyramid instead of its eastern part. While the design has been reconstructed in a few places however, a massive shaft tomb destroyed a large portion of the temple in its Saite Period. The main entrance of the temple was located at the southeast corner. Near the storerooms and an entry hall. Beyond that was an open, pillared courtyard composed of pink and basalt. The southern wall, was a huge statue of Userkaf 5 meters high and carved with pink granite. In the wake of The Great Sphinx, this is the largest known colossal sculpture from the Egyptian ruler. The pyramid of cult was located at the southwest corner the entire complex. In addition, the whole complex was enclosed by a wall. [79]

The decrepit Pyramid of Userkaf with the Step Pyramid in the background

Sahure constructed his pyramid structure in Abusir like numerous other of his successors. It is worth noting that this was also the location where Userkaf constructed his sun temple, which is discussed in the following paragraphs. Despite the poor conservation of the actual pyramid it is among the best preserved complexes of pyramids in Egypt. It also marks the first to be standardized in pyramid complexes that include an established layout for the temple of pyramids. The temple of the pyramid is located on the eastern side of the pyramid. It also had an entry hall (per-wer) and the courtyard was columned, as well as the chapel, which had five niches, large storerooms along with an offering chamber. The Eighteenth Dynasty, the columned courtyard served as a site to worship the Goddess Sekhmet who was a very preserved relief sculpture. In the beginning of Christian times the courtyard was utilized for religious purposes but this time it was to house an erected Coptic shrine. [82]

Pyramid of Sahure Pyramid of Sahure

In 1994 In 1994, in 1994, the Egyptian Supreme Council of Antiquities made a decision to partially reconstruct Sahure's complex to open it to the general public. This resulted in the exploration of previously unexplored parts, especially the causeway, which revealed huge blocks that had unique designs. Valley temples are one the few remaining and is located on the quays that has a columned entrance hall, and an inside space with a niche for a statue. The valley temple was divided into two parts an aspect that has been unable to be explained. Both the pyramid and valley temples were covered with relief decorations, a large part of which is still preserved. The cemetery is situated just north of the, was built in the time of Sahure and is believed to be the place where his close relatives were interred. [85]

Neferirkare's pyramid is the biggest one at Abusir however the pyramid and its surrounding complex never got completed. The pyramid was initially constructed as a step-pyramid with six steps , but was later transformed into the true pyramid. There were a few rooms in the pyramid temple were built with stone prior to the moment of the death of the king however the vast majority of the complex needed to be built with mudbrick. The limestone, which was the oldest parts of the temple's pyramid were the most inner, sacred rooms on the east-facing side of the pyramid including an offering chamber, 3 smaller chambers as well as the chapel with five niches. There was no cult pyramid was constructed, but there were pits for boats that contained large wooden vessels within areas of courtyards within the complex. The causeway as well as the valley temples were taken over by Niuserre. The causeway being diverted to his own complex of pyramids. [90]

Neferirk's Pyramid Pyramid of Neferirkare

A huge collection of administrative papyri was discovered in the temple of the pyramid of Neferirkare. The papyri were not found through an archaeological expedition however, they were discovered through grave robbers digging illegally from the early 1890s. The papyri detail the day-to-day management of the complex, and provide specific details of the way in which the complex operated. [91]

The next pyramid to Neferirkare's was the palace of the queen who was Khentkawes II. Khentkawes I had been the maternal grandmother of Neferirkare and was the spouse of Shepseskaf. Her tomb is located in a huge mastaba located in Giza. [92] The queen who was second in line, Khentkawes, was the spouse of Neferirkare and mother of Neferefre as well as Niuserre. Her pyramid was a similar, but smaller complex of pyramids that was not completed. In the remains of the tomb excavation workers found a small piece of the pink granite sarcophagus pieces of mummy wraps, and fragments of stone vessels taken from the queen's burial apparatus which indicates that the pyramid was used to hold her funeral before the thieves cleared it. The pyramid's inscriptions suggest that it was built under the Neferirkare regime but completed during the rule of Khentkawes' son. [93]

Raneferef (or Neferefre [94or Neferefre[94) was the first to begin building his pyramid in Abusir however, at the time of the time of his death, the pyramid consisted of only an excavation shaft that had an approach ramp as well as one of the courses that formed the pyramid's core. The tomb was quickly constructed as a mastaba or truncated pyramid. It also had an occult-like structure on the eastern end serving just as the temple at the pyramid could have been. The limestone parts of this small cult house could have been designed as the central part of a temple and later transformed into an entirely new cult structure. The cult temple was discovered to house administrative papyri like the ones located in the temple of Neferirkare.

Despite the plundering, an archeological team in the 1970s discovered fragments of the sarcophagus of pink granite and pieces of four canopic alabaster containers, alabaster containers to hold offerings as well as parts of the mummy belonging to the King. The analysis revealed that the monarch was aged between and twenty-three when the time he passed away. The king's age was young at the time of his death. is the reason the king was not able to finish his pyramid within the time frame. [96]

Niuserre's pyramid was built in Abusir however, its interior is damaged by quarrying stone. The site was probably chosen in order because it was close to former family members, however, in the time of Niuserre, the possibilities for a new location of the pyramid in Abusir were very limited. The idea of pushing the complex deeper into the desert was too costly and so the pyramid was constructed in a tiny area bordered by Neferirkare's temple of the dead Sahure's Pyramid, several massive mastabas dating from in the early days in the Fifth Dynasty. The entryway to the pyramid was located on the surface on the north-facing. Borchardt didn't find any evidence of a chapel in the north but he probably did not search for it and could have not seen any remains. Within this pyramid was the hallway leading to the chamber of burial was covered with pink granite and white limestone. The antechamber and the burial chamber were so severely damaged from stone thieves, that they're difficult to rebuild. The pyramid temple was built in two distinct sections, probably because of a insufficient space. The cult pyramid was located in the southeast corner.[102] Likewise, the southeast and northeast corners were converted into massive fortified bastions. However, it is unclear what the reason was. It is possible that they could be the precursors of massive pylons that were found in earlier Egyptian temples. The basalt-paved courtyard had papyrus columns within the corridors around. The causeway, and possibly the valley temple were built on foundations that were laid by Neferirkare. The valley temple was a complex with two entrances, similar to that of Sahure and also had three shrines to the statue sanctuary. [106]

The lack of space in Abusir is no surprise that Djedkare instead constructed his complex of pyramids at South Saqqara. The foundation of his pyramid was constructed in a different way than the earlier pyramids. It was comprised of smaller, irregular pieces of limestone joined using clay mortar. This was in contrast to earlier times when the use of larger stones for the core. The entrance was located on the road on the north-facing side, beneath the chapel in the north. Inside the pyramid the main funerary rooms had three rooms rather than the two that were standard. Alongside the burial chamber and the antechamber there was also an additional room that contained storage niches. The burial chamber used to have an enormous sarcophagus made composed of dark grey basalt, which was located near the west wall, however only fragments of the sarcophagus as well as the canopic jars made of alabaster were able to escape stones robbers. The mummy of the King was found in the rubble and was around fifty years old at the time it was discovered that he had died. The pyramid temple was the first one to use a particular spatial layout, which would later be replicated in all subsequent pyramids from The Old Kingdom. Although earlier pyramid temples had numerous of these elements this appears to be the model which would be repeated repeatedly. On both sides of the temple's pyramid are bastions that resemble the ones in Niuserre's complex. Both the causeway as well as valley temples are located, but they have not been discovered. The northeastern part of the temple is a smaller complex of pyramids that could be the work of an unknown queen or the successor of Djedkare. [109]

Pyramid of Djedkare-Isesi Pyramid of Djedkare-Isesi

The pyramid of Unas is most well-known for being the first pyramid to include the famous pyramid text in its chamber walls. The texts will be further discussed below. The structure itself is small, and smaller than the other pyramids from that of the fifth and sixth dynasties likely due to the lack of resources. The pyramid's entrance was under the north chapel which was a small room that contained a stela as well as an alter in the form that of an offer table. The structure had three chambers like the one at Djedkare in addition, the tomb was adorned with an sarcophagus made of black basalt in the middle of a painted royal palace façade. A canopic chest was initially put in a niche the floor to the southeast of the sarcophagus. However, it was removed along with the majority of the items from the tomb were taken by thieves. A few fragments of the mummy remain as well as a few of smaller objects. [110]

Pyramid of Unas and the Pyramid of Unas

The pyramid temple is built on the standard plan for these types of temples, and is decorated with palm columns made of granite in the courtyard [111] and an entrance with names of Teti and indicating how the temple of Unas was built during the time by his son. The causeway measures 666 m [113] in length and has a variety of changes in direction probably because it was a relic of earlier structures and also avoiding earlier built structures along the path. A few structures were destroyed for the causeway, like the superstructures that housed the notorious "tomb of two brothers" or "tomb of the hairdressers"" Niankhkhnum and Khnumhotep. Large portions of the relief design of the causeway have been preserved , or are capable of being rebuilt and features market scenes as well as hunter scenes, hungry enemies as well as battle scenes as well as other battle scenes. [115] In the process of examining the temple in the valley and the valley temple, the archeologist Dr. Ahmed Moussa discovered a greywacke sarcophagus that was found on the terrace in front of the temple that contained the burial mummy of the prince Ptahshepses. [116] It could have been removed from the tomb of his to safeguard it from tomb thieves. Two of his wives had mastabas to the northeast of his pyramid instead of smaller pyramids. A large portion of the relief and stone found throughout the Unas's complex were reused by later structures, such as Amenemhat's pyramid complex in Lisht (Twelfth Dynasty) as well as the structures from Tanis (Twenty-first and twenty-second dynasties). [117]

The Sixth Dynasty

The Sixth Dynasty began under the regime of Teti. The pyramid of Teti was similar as Djedkare's. It is the most northern complex of pyramids built at Saqqara. The structure was identical to that of Unas's pyramid as was the entry point, located beneath the chapel in the north. The burial chamber as well as the antechamber are adorned with pyramidal texts and the ceiling mimics the night sky with stars and the same decor was seen inside the pyramids of Unas. The temple of the pyramid is in accordance with the standard plan The valley temple and causeway are not yet discovered. The cult temple is situated in the southeast portion of the complex and within the courtyard's pavement close by were quartzite basins used to be used for the libations. Within the pyramid are a number of massive tombs that include Queens Khuit as well as Iput I as well as those of the viziers Mereruka as well as Kagemni. Khuit as well as Iput I each had their own small pyramids. Iput I's structure was initially constructed as a mastaba, but it was changed into a pyramid during rule of her son, Pepi I. The remains of an older woman were discovered within, as were pieces of the queen's funerary apparatus. [121]

Pyramid of Teti. Pyramid of Teti

Text inscriptions in a picture in the burial chamber.

Pepi I built his pyramid complex in South Saqqara, near the pyramid of Djedkare. The name Pepi's pyramid was is Men-nefer-Pepi. It means "Pepi's beauty and goodness endures." The village that was nearby soon came to be known under the names of both the Pyramid, and the town of the pyramid, which was named Men-nefer which is also Memphis or Memphis in Greek. A second restoration text written by Khamwaset indicates that the structure was excellent condition in the Nineteenth Dynasty, requiring little maintenance, which is why most of the damage to the structure has taken place since then. The remains of the chapel in the north, though it may have been located over the entrance of the pyramid. The pyramid's substructure follows the layout standard for the time, and so does the temple of the pyramid. Only a few pieces of the burial equipment originally used were discovered. Six smaller pyramids were found in the south of the main pyramid probably being the property of queens. [123]

Its pyramid, Merenre was also constructed at South Saqqara. Inside the structure were an sarcophagus made of black basalt and a canopic chest. The reliefs on the walls of pyramid mortuary temples are not finished. The overall condition of the pyramid isn't known and is in poor shape in the present. Incredibly, The (auto)biography of an official identified as Weni from Abydos discusses the acquisition of a variety of items for the complex of pyramids. He was sent to the quarry in Nubia for the sarcophagus , and the pyramidion, as well as to Aswan to purchase an offering table made of granite door jambs, door jambs and Lintels. [126]

Pepi II is most well-known for his long rule (94 days) as well as his pyramid, which was the only one to be built in the Old Kingdom to be built with the standard pyramid arrangement. The pyramid of Pepi II is located next to the Mastabat El-Fara'un in South Saqqara. A lot of relief decorations have kept from the temple of the pyramid and includes pictures that depict and the Sed festival, which was a celebration dedicated to the god Min as well as the execution of an execution of a Libyan chieftain, the latter of which was clear copying scenes from earlier ones like those found in the temple of the pyramid in Sahure. [128The southeast and northeast areas of the temple were constructed as bastions which were similar to earlier temple pylons. Reliefs of the temple in valley were preserved, as well as depicting battle scenes and victories over Egyptian enemies and the king being accepted in the presence of the gods. In the vicinity of this complex were the complexes of the pyramids of the three queens of Pepi II's queens. They also shared with the smaller structure of Qakare Ibi who was an eighth dynasty king to be further discussed below. [130]

Chapter 8: Sun Temples and Pyramid Texts

Sun temples were a breakthrough from their time during the Fifth Dynasty. Six of the seven rulers from this period have been credited to have constructed temples: Userkaf, Sahure, Neferirkare, Raneferef, Niuserre and Menkauhor. The temples are mostly identified by the textual evidence that includes the titularies of the priests who were their servants. The temples at Userkaf and Niuserre have been discovered archaeologically. [131]

First sun temple was constructed by Userkaf, is located in Abusir in the to the north of Saqqara. His pyramid is located in north Saqqara which means that the two were close in proximity. Niuserre's sun temple was constructed in Abu Ghurab, north of Abusir which is the site of his pyramid. While the location of other sun temples aren't yet known, it is possible that Sahure's sun-temple was in Abusir because many of the blocks bearing the name of his sun temple were discovered reused in the bastions of the Niuserre's pyramid complex. It's unclear if the blocks are remnants of the construction of the shrine or the structure was destroyed prior to the construction of Niuserre's pyramid structure. It is likely that the remains from a massive granite obelisk found on the site belonged to Sahure's Sun Temple also. [132]

It appears that the sun temples were typically constructed near to the complex of the pyramids of the King. This in conjunction with their resemblance to funerary monuments suggests the purpose of mortuary for these temples. The sun temples had the principal temple as well as a causeway and valley temple that was similar to a pyramid structure. The main temple was an open court that had an obelisk in the center mounted on a huge pedestal. The temples were built using mudbricks, and then transformed into stone. Userkaf's temple did not have any reliefs on the walls, however Niuserre's had wall reliefs. The monuments are described as "personal memorials to each monarch's connection with sun gods in afterlife."[135 They were dedicated to the god of the sun and also to his son the King. [136]

Temples had their own priests, staff and cults as well as the land needed to support the cults. It is interesting that these sun temples were incorporated into the economy of the country, so that the products produced were usually to support the sun temples as well as the pyramid cults of deceased monarchs however, they would later be employed to aid the population in general. Priesthood appointments in sun temples could be solely in title, which allowed them to benefit from the office, for instance, the ability to lease temple land. [137]

According to the textual evidence the last king to construct an Sun temple is Menkauhor. As mentioned above we don't know the location of his pyramid complex situated, so we don't know where his sun temple nearby was. However, some priests who were associated with his cult were linked to the region of southern Abusir as well as North Saqqara, suggesting that his sun temple and the pyramid complex might have been close there. [138]

One can't write a story of the pyramids of Egypt without mentioning the texts of pyramids. The texts of the pyramids were discovered in tombs of ten queens and kings: Unas (Dynasty 5), Teti (Dynasty 6), Pepi I (Dynasty 6), Ankhesenpepi (wife of Pepi I Dynasty 6) Merenre (Dynasty 6), Pepi II (Dynasty 6), Neith (wife of Pepi II Dynasty 6), Iput II (wife of Pepi II Dynasty 6,), Wedjebetni (wife of Pepi II Dynasty 6) and the Ibi (Dynasty 8.). These are the first religious texts found in Egypt and could be the oldest written work in Egypt. At the time of the end period of the Old Kingdom, these texts were also put on tombstones such as coffins, canopic chests papyri and stelae which were both belonging to the royal as well as nonroyal

Egyptians. As the usage of these texts increased and additional texts appeared which is why the corpus became often referred to as The Coffin Texts[140] because of their placement on this object of the funerary assemblage. [141]

In the texts of the pyramids the dead king is frequently called Osiris as an image that of God of Death. Certain spells are addressed to the dead and were probably intended to be read by a priest or lector during funeral ceremonies. By etching these spells onto burial walls, they could be guaranteeing the efficacy of funeral rituals throughout the duration of time. The spells were also composed in first person created so that the dead could utilize them to direct his travels in the afterlife and to ward off any evil forces that might try to cause harm to the deceased. In general, there is a particular emphasis on the deceased's relationship to Osiris god of death and Ra god of the sun. Both of which were crucial for the funerary religion of the time. [142]

Chapter 9: The Royal Tombs After the Sixth Dynasty

Following the fall in the Sixth Dynasty, the country's administration was in chaos. There are numerous theories on what caused this to happen however the main point is that the rulers of subsequent First Intermediate Period had neither the authority nor the assets of their Old Kingdom predecessors. So, it's not unusual to find their graves from the grandiose structures of those of the Old Kingdom pyramid complexes. In the case of the majority of the kings of this period, no one is aware of the exact location of their tombs, even assuming that their short reigns as monarchs of the time permitted them to construct the proper tomb. Certain texts indicate that different rulers from the final days of Old Kingdom and the First Intermediate Period have built pyramids, however the majority of them are not found. One pyramid, dubbed

Headless Pyramid Headless Pyramid in North Saqqara could have been the property of King Merikare of in the Heracleopolitan Period. [144]

It is believed that King Qakare Ibi from King Qakare II of Eighth Dynasty is the rare exception to the rule. His small , solitary pyramid in South Saqqara is not only the only monumental tomb recognized from this time It is also the sole source for royal pyramid texts prior to that of the Sixth Dynasty. The pyramid texts provide the name of the king without a doubt regarding the identity of the owner of the pyramid. The pyramid is largely destroyed by stone thieves however, the inside has the same layout as other pyramids dating from the last days of the Old Kingdom. [146]

While not a pyramid, another worth mentioning is a huge massive tomb located in Dara located in Middle Egypt. The decay of the structure makes it difficult to determine whether it was an ancient one-piece or an encased mastaba however, the substructure is more akin the early mastababas of the dynastic period rather than later Old Kingdom pyramids. The only indication of the tomb's owner was not located inside the tomb it, but in the nearby tomb in which the cartouche of an unidentified ruler Khui was found. It is likely that he was an aristocratic local ruler during in the First Intermediate Period. [147]

The Middle Kingdom Renaissance period in every sense. Not only was the old wisdom revived and reused, but new ideas and inventions were abundant. Architecturally, royal tombs went through modifications that brought about new inventions and a return to traditional pyramidal shape.

In The Eleventh Dynasty centered at Thebes, Mentuhotep managed to reunite all in Egypt under one king. Due to the significance of this achievement and the importance of his accomplishment, it's not surprising that he would have an impressive and monumental tomb. The temple in Deir el-Bahri was both his funeral temple as well as a temple dedicated to Theban gods, particularly Montu-Ra, [148the goddess Hathor as well as the God Amun. The kings prior to The Eleventh Dynasty were buried nearby at El-Tarif in tombs of saff. [151 It is believed that the Deir el-Bahri temple was a totally new invention, but it was a mix of local saff tombs as well as items previously housed in pyramid temples or complexes. This temple was crucial in the change between to the Old Kingdom pyramid temple to the "houses of millions of years" during the New Kingdom. It also maintained its status as an important place of worship for many future generations, which is the reason Hatshepsut from the Eighteenth Dynasty built her temple close to the.

The mortuary temple was surrounded by its own causeway leading to a valley temple similar to the kind of pyramid that any feature. The causeway was about 1200m long and millimeters wide, which was enough to hold the annual festival procession of cult symbols. The temple was terraced and open in front and contained halls with pillars. The front of the structure was dedicated to Montu-Ra. It comprised a core structure that was built on the terrace. The the top on the center core was an elongated pyramid, possibly an earthen mound intended to represent the mound of the primeval period, or an altar for the sun that was similar to those of the Fifth Dynasty sun temples. The temple's walls were decorated with the style of Memphite styles, and featured themes like those of Old Kingdom pyramid temples, including hunting and battle. It was the most recent stage of decorating the temple (earlier periods were more in line with the local Theban style) and the themes were based on some rituals and customs of the local community. [156]

The rear part in the temple is dedicated for the god of the King. The area was cut into the cliff's face, comprised of a courtyard the pillared hall, as well as a statue chapel. The tomb of the king was dug deeper in the mountain. its entrance to the temple being through the inner part in the shadow of the statue chapel. The chapel housed a bigger than life cult of the King. The tomb, carved 150m deep in the mountain, contained an alabaster statue of the king inside an enormous granite chamber. Within this altar was a coffin made of wood to be used for the burial of the King. A second tomb was also cut out of the lower courtyard, however the tomb was only an image of the king, and an unfilled coffin. It was probably the first tomb constructed by the king. Later, it was substituted with the burial chamber within the mountain, and this was the reason why it was originally an osiris-themed burial site. Osiris, the goddess of death. Osiris. Temple of Montuhotep was home to the burials of several royal women, the wives of his priestesses and wife Hathor. The burials of these women provide scholars and archaeologists with a amount of information about the roles played by women of the royal family during this time period, as well as their involvement in the worship of Hathor. [160]

The tombs of two rulers following Montuhotep I - Montuhotep III as well as Montuhotep IV have not been discovered archaeologically. In the time of Amenemhat I, Egyptian kings once again began to build pyramids for their forever resting place.

Following his accession to the throne and thus establishing the Twelfth Dynasty, Amenemhat I[161started building a huge tomb in Thebes close to the tomb of Montuhotep II in Deir el-Bahri. In 162 however Amenemhat I soon made the decision to relocate not just his tomb place, but also his capital of the country to north. The capital of this time that was known to the ancients as Itji Tawy,[163] hasn't yet been discovered archaeologically, however, it is likely to be far from the location of Lisht which was the place where Amenemhat constructed his pyramid tomb.

The Amenemhat I pyramid Amenemhat I at Lisht North was, in a way, innovative, since it was constructed using several traditional Theban elements, as well as number of the traditions that were found in the later Sixth Dynasty pyramids. The complex was constructed using blocks from several older pyramid temples, such as Khufu, Khafre, Userkaf, Unas, and Pepi II. The structure that is in use today was not the first pyramid that was designed for the King. A previous pyramid was clearly demolished then reused within the new complex and the pyramid together with elements of other complexes that were mentioned. It's not surprising that it was a common practice for him to reuse elements from his earlier complex, possibly in the same region in the same area as Lisht North, however it is not clear what the motive behind his reuse of stone from different distant monuments, particularly when it is not clear if he could have taken elements from other nearby landmarks e.g. at Dahshur. [165]

The older pyramid was believed to have a pyramid-style temple, based on archeological features that were discovered, however the current pyramid was the statue cult temple. The temple as well as the entire pyramid were constructed by Senwosret I who was at least partially in the time of his coregency together with his father Amenemhat I. Reliefs that are associated with the temple exhibit a variety of styles, which highlight both the creativity and archaism of the time. [167]

The structure of Senwosret I in Lisht South was more closely aligned with the traditional Late Old Kingdom pyramid complex model. The temple of the pyramid did not contain the many storage spaces that were typical of Old Kingdom predecessors, but the overall design was very identical. The reliefs on the temple's walls were of the same style and heavily inspired by the Memphite customs from the latter part of the Old Kingdom. The complex featured two enclosure walls. Not just the usual outer enclosure wall, but there was also an inside wall that separated the king's palace from the other nine pyramids that were in the enclosure's outer. The wall inside was decorated with representations of the King's Horus name in the form of a palace's façade. The causeway was lined with statue pillars, which linked the palace to the king's Sed Festival celebration. [170]

Nearby, the monument that was Senwosret It was where I found the huge graveyard of an official whose name was Senwosretankh ("Senwosret lives"). This tomb featured a huge superstructure adorned with a palace façade. Inside the tomb wall of the chamber is engraved with pyramidal texts, much as royal tombs from earlier times. Old Kingdom. [171]

Amenemhat II built his pyramid in Dahshur and the structure is known today by the name of "White Pyramid" due to its color. limestone rubble. The pyramid and the surrounding complex has been extensively destroyed. Architecturally, the structure of the pyramid is distinctive in the more complex use of slabs that relieved weight that protected the entrance passageway as well as the burial chamber against massive weight of the pyramid to the top. It also stands out in that it was built on a platform, possibly to form a solid foundation. The sarcophagus was buried in the foundation in the chamber of burial. It was comprised out of huge quartzite slabs. [172]

Senwosret II made the decision to construct his pyramid near to the Faiyum in Lahun. This could be because of the growing curiosity about and around the Faiyum throughout that Middle Kingdom period. [173] The most significant attraction of the site for modern scholars isn't the actual pyramid but the town that is located nearby as discussed below. The pyramid's entrance is not located situated on the north of the pyramid like most of the time it is instead hidden within the burial chamber of a queen's tomb. The burial chamber of the king includes a sarcophagus separate from the rock surrounding it, which is a nod to the legend about Osiris along with the mound beneath the sarcophagus where his body parts were laid to rest. The complex is comprised of an inner enclosure with a niche composed of limestone. It also has a second sacred pyramid, the substructure of which hasn't yet been discovered. The pyramid temple was totally destroyed. The site was enclosed by 42 trees which again connected the complex with the mythology of Osiris. The temple in the valley is located within the town of the pyramid, but it isn't believed to have been linked to the complex by any kind of causeway. Private tombs are scattered around the area, as does an unmarked tomb (621) that Arnold suggests could have been a second tomb of the King. Nearby were burial sites that belonged to royal families, such as that of the notorious Sithathoriunet. Her beautiful jewelry, including pieces of precious stones and gold are renowned throughout the world. Her jewelry did not only contain names like Senwosret II, which is likely to be her father as well as her names,

Senwosret III, and Amenemhat III which suggests that she lived through their reigns too. [176]

The city of pyramids in Lahun was well-preserved enough to produce designs for domestic architecture, large array of domestic artifacts and an abundance of very important papyri. A detailed discussion of the town and other planned settlements is not the subject of this essay,[177however, it is important to note that the town's importance was in the understanding of the pyramids and royal mortuary cults from the past of Egypt.

the reign of Senwosret III is an important turning point within the Middle Kingdom. The reign of Senwosret III generally marked the division in two kingdoms: the "Early Middle Kingdom" and the "Late Middle Kingdom." Senwosret III, as numerous other kings, built multiple tombs for himself. He had an ancient pyramid in Dahshur and an ingenuous burial place at Abydos.

Senwosret III's Pyramid at Dahshur is similar to the earlier complexes of pyramids, but added some features that were not present in earlier pyramids. The complex was surrounded by an inner and outer enclosure walls with niches. The entrance to the pyramid was concealed to the west, as was the tomb, which was a part of the largest granite sarcophagus. The temple in the pyramid located on the east of the pyramid was tiny in comparison to other temples. However, the complex contained the largest stone temple dedicated to the cult of the King in the south, referred to by the name of"the South Temple. The causeway went through this temple first before it entered the other parts of the complex. The complex is comprised of seven other pyramids, which includes the one for Queen Weret II who's tomb contained exquisite jewelry. Two galleries located north of the pyramid contained tombs of several queens who were interred with stunning jewellery pieces. The jewelry of the princesses Merit and Sithathor is particularly well-known.

Although many have thought there was a possibility that the burial site at Abydos was merely a tombstone for the king Senwosret III Josef Wegner has convincingly suggested that it could be the final resting location. He also has proven that the tomb was the predecessor of The Valley of the Kings tombs of the New Kingdom and the royal Amduat style tomb. The tomb was constructed under the aforementioned mountain, which Wegner along with others suggest was intended to symbolize the natural pyramid. The tomb was constructed deep within the gebel and was covered in white limestone and sections of red quartzite that represented connections to the gods Osiris as well as Ra. The tomb's exterior was a huge funerary enclosure as well as the mortuary temple, which was located closer in proximity to Nile (like an avalon temple) as well as the site's own "pyramid" city, Wah-Sut.

Amenemhat III built his first pyramid in Dahshur which is now is known as Dahshur, also known as "Black Pyramid", beginning construction on the structure early during his reign. It was good that he began construction early, as the pyramid was not strong enough to serve as the burial site of the king's last burial site. The substructure was extremely complicated comprising an burial chamber, the granite sarcophagus as well as a Ka tomb, and an antechamber that was a staggering fifteen for the king, as well as elaborate complexes to accommodate two queens with its individual burial chamber, antechamber and the ka tomb. However, the pyramid was unstable and the interior chambers were badly damaged in the course of construction it was subsequently removed to be replaced by a brand new Hawara complex, which is discussed further below.

The complex of the pyramids had the valley temple, as well as boat pits. In the remains of the temple to the pyramid was discovered a gorgeous black basalt pyramid that was inscribed to the King. To the north in the pyramid was an unfinished tomb of the Thirteenth Dynasty king, Hor Awibre. The king was obviously not rich or powerful enough to afford his own massive tomb, so he tried to link his tomb with that of the Amenemhat III pyramid. Amenemhat III.

Amenemhat III's newest pyramid located at Hawara is well-known for the huge temple that was connected to it, which was written about in the works of Herodotus, Strabo, and Diodorus. The temple was often similar to the labyrinth at Knossos due to its enormous dimensions and complexity, hence it is called"the "labyrinth." The present day structure is totally destroyed to the point that reconstruction is not possible. The actual pyramid was more sturdy than the Dahshur predecessor. The burial chamber for the king was built from one quartzite block and weighing more than 100 tons. [180]

Following the reign of Amenemhat III, the power of the royal family began to fall in to decline. Amenemhat IV ruled only for nine months, which could be due to the advancing age of his predecessors after the long rule by his father. It is not known much about his reign. However, Amenemhat IV appears to have been succeeded by his spouse and his sister Queen Sobekneferu. Like the later Queen Hatshepsut employed female and male titles to be able to accept her new role. She was known to have included the Labyrinth of Amenemhat III among other monuments. A statue of her has not been found, but the images we have reveal a ambiguity of gender. Both her tomb and the one of Amenemhat IV aren't identified as archeologically. [181]

Following the demise of Twelfth Dynasty, power of the Egyptian monarchs again decreased. The earliest kings of the Thirteenth Dynasty still upheld the Middle Kingdom rule, but after this dynastyended, Egypt entered into the Second Intermediate Period, torn between the

Egyptian monarchs as well as their successors, the Hyksos of the northern region, as well as the growing influence from Kerma from the South. This is why many Kings of the time didn't have the means to build massive tombs that reflected the ancient customs of their predecessors.

The Thirteenth Dynasty king Khendjer built the complex of a pyramid located in South Saqqara. The pyramidion with black-colored decoration of this structure has been discovered by Jequier. The sarcophagus is made of quartzite and the lid alone was 60 tonnes. The temple of a small pyramid was situated east of the pyramid, and there was a chapel north. The wall of the enclosure was made of niched limestone like those of the earlier Middle Kingdom kings. A pyramid for the queen was situated in the northeast part of the complex, which contained a substructure, with two chambers for burial. [182]

The southwest of Khendjer's pyramid is another pyramidthat is unfinished, probably dating back from the Thirteenth Dynasty. The identity of the owner is not known however, many of the architectural elements have a similarity to Khendjer's Pyramid, such as channels of sand that could be utilized to reduce the lid of the sarcophagus and this time, a piece of 150 tons of quartzite. The structure of the pyramid comprises not just an actual burial space as well as an antechamber for the king, but also a smaller burial chamber that could have been used by queens. Two granite pyramids were discovered near the entry point of the pyramid. The pyramid was evidently left incomplete, since it is surrounded by a curving and wavy wall that is that is typical for "in-progress" building sites found in the old Egypt. [184]

Chapter 10: The Unification

It was about 3100 B.C. when the King Menes was the capital of ancient Egypt was located at was located at the White Walls which was later named Memphis. This was located in the north, near the apex Nile Delta of the Nile. The capital would eventually grow into a thriving metropolis that was ruled by the Egyptian society during the time that was known as that of the Old Kingdom. This time period, commonly known as "Archaic" also saw a variety of advancements in the foundations of society, including the notion of the king's role. In the eyes of many early Egyptians King was considered to be a godlike person and was closely associated with Horus. It is important to remember that some of the earliest hieroglyphs which have been discovered can be traced back to this time.

In this time, as the preceding in the past, the majority of the early Egyptians lived in small , isolated villages. Agriculture was the main source of income of the state, and the annual floods of the Nile in actual fact offered them the much-needed irrigation and fertilization each year. Farmers would plant wheat once the flood had diminished and would then go on to harvest it right before the hot temperatures in which droughts mark its return.

After we've got the fundamentals covered, let's discuss the extent to which they prospered. The time of the Pyramid Builders, which was about 2686 B.C., is also thought as a gold period for stability and peace. The pharaohs possessed the complete power and were capable of providing an unshakeable central government for the entire kingdom. There were no significant threats from any of the countries and they conducted successful campaigns across various foreign nations, including Libya and Nubia All of which helped to boost the already booming business of Egypt. Also, it was in this period that the pyramids were constructed that are now one of the most famous monuments to this ancient civilization.

In fact, it was the King Djoser who gave the order to Imhotep the priest, architect, healer and architect to design, for him the funerary monument. The result was the first stone structure and the pyramid of Saqqara located near Memphis. It was, however not the first or the last of the type. Numerous structures have been constructed following it, and the construction of these structures reached its peak at the time that it was the time that Great Pyramid at Giza was built. It is located on the outskirts of Cairo It was constructed to honor Khufu who was the ruler of in the kingdom of 2589 B.C. until 2566 B.C.

It was the one that the ancient historians believed to be one of the seven wonders of ancient times in the world. It is surrounded by two other structures he constructed to honor his successors. While not as spectacular as Khufu's, they're equally impressive. Similar to other civilizations power and wealth are often displayed in the structures they constructed. The pyramids certainly served as an emblem of the country's immense wealth and prosperity, though the pyramids did not be sustained for long and this was partly because of the structure itself.

In the fifth and the sixth dynasties, kingdom's wealth gradually diminished. The power of the king was shattered against the increasing power of the clergy as well as the nobility that were forged by the Sun god Ra. The kingdom fell into chaos following the death of the King Pepy the II's death, the ruler for a total of period of 94 years. He was the ruler in the sixth Dynasty.

Chapter 11 Giza: The Great Pyramid located at Giza

The motive behind these grand structures was fairly simple, similar to the pharaohs that have gone before him. Khufu simply wanted to build a lavish "house of the future" in his own home for. Perhaps one of the most fascinating facts about their construction however, is that the planning began when the pharaoh ascended over the reigns. He certainly looked ahead, in a sense. The site was chosen because of a particular reason. Cemeteries were typically built on the west side of the Nile and this is because it was believed that the sun "died" in the western horizon every time it was nighttime.

We must not forget that they're a highly superstitious people.

The Khufu's architects were experts, knowledgeable of the ancient traditions, and knew how important it was to the construction of these structures. This is why they made sure that the sides facing east, north, and west. The largest pyramid ever designed and constructed. The outlines of the pyramid were initially marked with sand dunes and then from there, construction was started. Massive stone blocks that were carved from nearby quarries were carried across the desert towards the construction site. A variety of groups of men as well as slaves had been "employed" to carry out this. Some of them were farmers who earned a living during the time of floods by building the pyramid.

After the initial layer of blocks were set in place, the builders created ramps made of clay, mud as well as limestone chip. They moved the stones across the ramps to construct the next layer of the structure. This was quite ingenuous, in fact it was carried out at an era when there was not much technology was in use. It was an extremely hard and tiring work. This is why the building took over 20 years to complete and hundreds of workers worked on the structure, using the same idea frequently - ramps for each levels.

The pyramid was getting close to its completion, a particular block, covered in shiny material (whether it was electrum or gold it is not known) was erected at the highest point. For its cover the limestone, white was cut to ensure that the exterior of the pyramid appeared uniform and smooth. The pyramid, however, is only one part of the entire complex that was constructed at Giza. There are numerous other parts including:

Three pyramids that were built to honor his queens.

A number of deep pits were intended to house boats that were buried together with the Pharaoh.

A temple of the dead in which he could be worshipped in the event of his death.

A causeway that connects the complex of pyramids towards the temple in valley.

A valley temple, where the funeral would take place.

A smaller "satellite" pyramid.

The tombs of the mastaba were intended for the elite.

In Giza an additional intriguing structure is located and is as well-known as the other pyramids surrounding it. It's the grand Sphinx. It is a huge human-headed lion, created out of rock. It guards the very top of Khafra's Pyramid.

Many different stories have been made concerning this structure most of them focusing on its secrets and powers. Some believe that beneath it are hidden rooms and passageways that contain several treasures of great value and knowledge of the past of Egyptians themselves. But, nothing has been discovered yet. There is a tale about the Sphinx itself , which is in actual fact written on its feet.

The story is about the young prince that fell asleep beside the Sphinx. He was out all day hunting and was , therefore, very exhausted. In the evening night, he woke up dreaming that the Sphinx had offered him the supremacy over Upper and Lower Egypt if he was to get rid of the sand that was covering its body. At the time it was believed that it was believed that the Sphinx was covered in the sand that reached its neck. What happened to the promise? Did it become a reality? There is no way to know, as the remainder of the story. It has been long erased by the passage of time and sand.

But, if you look at who was the one who put the stele up then you may believe it was. This was the Egyptian king Thutmosis IV who lived in 1400 B.C.

Chapter 12: Inventions, Innovations and Technology

It's evident today, based on what we've learned about them, that the early Egyptians were definitely very advanced in their day. When compared with modern-day men, their achievements remain remarkable. We've had quite a long time to build computer technology, medical expertise and other technologies. The early Egyptians had much less time but they could make important contributions as well as inventions. The sundial was among them as well as the water clock were among the most notable. the capability to construct magnificent structures like the pyramids and their very own system of time. They certainly were ahead in comparison to other civilizations.

Let's talk about tools. Ancient Egyptians switched from copper to bronze tools when they found that they were more durable to work with. But, they substituted the bronze with iron about 200 BC since they were more robust. It was with these iron tools that they constructed a number of magnificent monuments and palaces. Of course it took longer as they were using hand tools rather than those we have today. But, it isn't difficult to see the genius they used to be. In the end, the remains of the pyramids and have been able to stand up to time and other forces that could destroy them. It's a testimony to how skilled their work was.

There were also calendars and clocks , though they were quite different from the ones we have today. There were ten days per week, and three weeks every month and approximately four months in each season. Each year saw three seasons, and the five days of holy day. All this amounts to a total of 365 days each year (this being among the greatest similarities). However this is still remarkable considering that not every civilization had a method of calculating the number of years.

The clocks of their time were quite different too. Actually, there were two distinct types. They are the solar clock and water clock. It sounds like a lot of work, however, in reality it's not. It's just a stand with a container on the top and another on bottom. The top one would be fitted with a hole in the side of it and then filled with water that is released onto the bottom one. It is basically, no matter what degree of water level it was the level at which it flowed. This was a great idea, but the only downside was the necessity to refill it regularly. the water.

The sundial is something you may all have seen. It's a circular ring surrounded by numbers and a stick in the middle. If the stick's shadow hits an exact number it is the moment.

In addition to the great pyramids, they were also the first to build obelisks. Egyptians also constructed other high structures, some of these can be seen. One of them is the Obelisks. The design of these was driven by the belief that If your name wasn't found at the time of your death and you were to disappear, then it would be impossible for you to come back. Because of this, everybody took the initiative to be buried somewhere. For the average person this is in their graves. But for those with the money and power of the Pharaohs, they had monuments constructed to ensure that they would be remembered. These monuments were as temples while others were the obelisk.

The ancient Egyptians have contributed more than magnificent monuments and buildings to the present day. They came up with many innovative ideas, one of the most popular is the practice of mummification. In reality, when we think of Egypt mummification is among the first items that pop into their minds and with good reason obviously. They're among the few civilizations who treated their dead with respect and, possibly, the only one to have the most advanced techniques for preservation. The process can happen from nature or be planned. Some are kept wet while others are dried or frozen.

However, the problem is, why do they do this? It's because of their convictions.

As a superstitious society They believed there are six elements that comprise human beings. That would include their physical body as well as their spirit, persona and their immortality. These elements are vital to the formation of a person. It is crucial if they wish to be reborn into the afterlife.

Chapter 13: Government and Military Power

In terms of their system of government the government was overseen by a single person and that person was the pharaoh. Naturally, in the past the ancient Egyptians believed that their King could be more powerful than a mere man. They believed that he was God and granted their ruler complete control over the entire kingdom as well as its citizens. In the past, Egypt was also governed by a theocracy that was ruled by the clergy. The pharaoh's advisers as well as the ministers were often not priests, who were believed to be the only individuals who were capable of fulfilling the orders of the king. Similar to other ancient societies similarly religious priests were able to earn an elevated status and were thought to be higher than the ordinary citizen. This was then a form of nobility.

The government officials also included the following items:

The vizier, also called the prime minister

The treasurer in chief

The minister responsible for public works

The tax collector

The commander of the army.

The officials all reported directly to the pharaoh directly. For the land they divided it into various provinces, which were known as nomes. Each nome had one person who was appointed to the role by the pharaoh who was their governor. He would report for his actions to the vizier.

Taxes were paid by goods as well as in labor. Citizens were also drafted into the military and forced to work for a set period of time to pay what's called corvee, also known as the tax on labor. The mercenaries, slaves and the ones who were drafted were available to the army. However, it is thought that Egyptian slaves weren't employed for the construction of many holy monuments. Many Egyptologists have come to this conclusion in the wake of the discovery of burial sites to workers working close to the monuments. The workers were buried in a proper manner but slaves did not.

The majority of this ancient population were in reality peasants that worked in on the fertile land that ran across the Nile. They had no kind of representation within the government and they simply accepted this due to the fact that they were an aspect of their religion. This fusion of the religion and government is believed to be one of the primary reasons for the reason Egypt was a powerful and centralized country during the golden age of Egypt.

Of course, any strong kingdom needs an army capable of defending itself against external influence. The Egyptian army, like most armies, was an outcome of the same society that brought it into existence. Although not particularly creative, as the Egyptians themselves are extremely traditional, they were adept at adapting the weaponry of their enemies and technology, creating an imposing force in the old world when it came to the use of force. Actually, they are thought by many to be the most powerful ever recorded.

But what are the weapons they carried?

The previous kingdom had soldiers armed with a variety of weapons, including maces, shields and spears and daggers, cudgels bows, and arrows. Battle axes and quivers first became popular in the first Intermediary Period. It was a period of change when it came to Egyptian fighting arts. The earliest archers that have been discovered could be traced from the 11th Dynasty. They were made of copper that was further tempered through the hammering. Of course they were not the only weapon that the impressive Egyptian army could offer.

The chariots will be able to pass through.

The classification of the chariot as military equipment is a challenge since it's often employed as a means of transportation on a daily basis. However, some experts suggest that it could be considered an instrument of war. Other civilizations also used it in this way, but the Egyptians used it in a different way. They utilized it to provide transportation for archers that were their stewards; thus it was primarily an aid when fighting. However, this doesn't mean they should be regarded as useless. They definitely gave the horse the edge in the battlefield.

For quite a long time the chariot was the means of transportation to the elite. It was used for conflicts or for religious issues that were related with the government. In the beginning it was pulled by a donkey. But, with the advent of the powerful horse there were some changes. This was the change that gave the impetus to the chariot, which later was a much more powerful weapon thanks to speed and endurance along with mobility. These attributes could not be achieved by the typical infantry. While its origins can be traced back to Asia however, the Egyptian chariot defied the lineage in a variety of ways. Its design and shape and most notably.

In the fifteenth century BC and during Pharaoh Tutmoses III's rule The kingdom was equipped with over 1000 chariots at their disposal. The number was soon to be exceeded in the reign of King Mitanni Great King Mitanni who boasted many times the amount. If you can consider the chariots lining up on an arena, and marching head into the direction of their foe, you will be able to consider the psychological effect it could have caused the soldiers. This was a sight that was not welcomed regardless of the force of an infantry.

Chapter 14: Mysteries and Secrets of the Ancients

There are many mysteries surrounding ancient Egypt. Some are believed to be nothing more than mere fiction, while others remain unsolved. For this section, we'll take a look at some the more intriguing ones which are certain to captivate.

Dendera Light bulb Dendera Light bulb There aren't many people realize this, but under the Temple of Hathor at Dendera it is possible to find tiny inscriptions that depict an object identical to contemporary light bulbs. Some have suggested that it's also reminiscent of the Crookes tube, which was a lightbulb from the early days. There are numerous theories about it, and there are many myths about the "bulbs" however they do not giving any real insight into the actual nature of it and what its purpose could have been.

The Mystery of Tutankhamun Did it actually occur? There are a myriad of theories. The sad thing lies in the fact that Howard Carter and his team were not very careful during the process of excavating his body during their investigation of the tomb. The unfortunate reality was that the team seemed more focused on getting rid of the jewelry and amulets which were hidden within the Tut's wraps, rather than taking care to ensure that the mummy was in good shape. In spite of this however, they still tried to determine the reason for death of the pharaoh. The x-rays have been taken that suggest a subdural hematoma that could be a possible cause of the death. But, it isn't confirmed.

The Exodus is among the most popular and controversial stories of the ancient Kingdom of Egypt. It is believed that the exodus story of people of the Jewish people is mentioned in the Bible but is often ignored by experts. What is the truth? What was the role of the Pharaoh at the time of the time?

As with the other mysteries of the old kingdom, it is a subject to a myriad of theories and ideas. The exodus is one thing to can be certain is the fact that beginning with the Twelfth dynasty and onwards there was a significant amount of Semitic people resided in Egypt and then emigrated out of the country to create Israel. Instead of the idea of a "great escape" as the Bible claims that it was a long and difficult journey through the desert, which was followed by the conquest of the military of Palestine.

Cleopatra was not Egyptian Like King Tut Another person who brings to mind whenever Egypt is mentioned could be Cleopatra VII. She was, however, not from Egyptian descent. She was actually from an extended family of Macedonians from Greece. She is related to Ptolemy I, among Alexander The Great's best respected lieutenants. A few people know this and, in actuality, many even argue about it until today.

Egyptians kept animals as instead of merely using animals for work or to eat, Egyptians regarded some of them with reverence and believed they were the Gods and Goddesses. They kept a variety of species like dogs, lions and Ibises. Cats were revered, and in actual fact, they were well-treated. The cats had a particular spot in the Egyptian home. They were frequently mummified and buried along together with their owners after they died.

The Egyptians made the first peace Treaties Ever Recorded - Although it's not uncommon today, peace treaties were not commonplace during the time of the early Egyptians. The Egyptiantreaty of Hittite agreement, signed around 1259 B.C. is recognized today to be one of the first peace agreements that are in force until the present day. Indeed, a copy of it is found right over the entry into the United Nations Security Council Chamber in New York. The point is that even those who were involved in a conflict which lasted for two centuries, eventually they can reach a consensus and bring peace to both countries this is something modern day men can take a lot of lessons from. There is a way to settle differences.

Conclusion

I want to thank you yet another time for purchasing this book. I hope you found it fascinating. I'm sure you did. Egyptian mythology and historical research are fascinating topics!

Don't forget, you don't have to stop your adventure to discover the secrets of Ancient Egypt by reading this book. A lot more has been written in order to assist you learn and appreciate the customs and practices of ancient Egyptians.

Thanks and best of luck!

www.ingramcontent.com/pod-product-compliance
Lightning Source LLC
Chambersburg PA
CBHW070908080526
44589CB00013B/1214